BEFORE Teaching and Learning:

A Principal's Playbook for Year One and Beyond

BEFORE Teaching and Learning:

A Principal's Playbook for Year One and Beyond

Chad E Gestson, Ed.D.

ISBN: 9781090347824

Table of Contents

Introduction

My wife and I began our careers in education in Phoenix, Arizona, in 2001, after having moved from Seattle to Phoenix through Teach For America. We still live and work in Phoenix and find ourselves more committed today to the success of under-resourced youth than ever before.

We have been very blessed in our now almost-20 years in education to have held most of the major roles that exist in school systems today – teacher, instructional coach, assistant principal, principal, professional development specialist, director, and superintendent. We have had great success and great failure. We have been surrounded by amazing educators and struggling ones. We have led small schools and large schools. We've led elementary schools, middle schools, and high schools. We've worked in three school districts, ranging from 6,000 students to nearly 30,000.

I now serve as the superintendent of Phoenix Union, the largest high school district in Arizona. Our district serves 28,000 students, most are low-income and minority. We believe our diversity is our biggest asset, and we are proud that our students come to us from nearly every continent and speak over 70 languages. We have 21 high schools in our portfolio – some are large (3,100 students) while others are intentionally designed to be small, specialty schools of less than 400 students. As a portfolio district, we are committed to providing our community a variety of schools that offer unique programs, pathways, and support structures. We know that not all learners thrive in the same environment.

Previously, I spent just over a year launching a new position in our district, the Director of School Leadership. This position, not that uncommon across the country, was designed to address three specific issues: principal supervision, professional development for leaders, and "pipelining" future assistant principals and principals. I'll explain briefly.

First, I was responsible for the oversight of principals. Unfortunately, supervision and guidance of school leaders is often an after-thought left to curriculum directors or superintendents, neither of whom have the time, or even the skills, to do so. From simple leadership dilemmas, such as preparing for a contentious parent meeting, to more difficult challenges like navigating bomb threats and student tragedies, principals need more support today than most districts currently provide.

Second, I facilitated professional development opportunities for all leaders. Finding ways to differentiate learning opportunities for over 100 leaders was (and still is) a very difficult task. First-year assistant principals and principals have much different needs than accomplished, veteran principals, let alone the middle-of-the-road mediocre leader. Our district, and many others, still continues to seek ways to reach all leaders.

Third, I was responsible for creating a pipeline of future assistant principals and principals. Developing a system to identify and select the best future leaders, lead them through learning and leadership opportunities to strengthen their skill set, and then launch them into their formal leadership careers has likely been the most rewarding of my leadership career.

An unexpected superintendent vacancy just two weeks into the school year pulled me away from the job that I anticipated serving in for many years to come. I am content but miss the real work.

Before moving to the district office, I served 10 years in campus administration. My first two years out of the classroom were spent as a K-5 assistant principal. I then spent three years as a middle school (5-8) principal. The final stop of my campus leadership journey was at the high school level where I spent five years leading a 2,000-student comprehensive urban high school. More on that later.

My wife, Megan, has also spent 18 years in education. She began her career as a middle school math teacher – not an easy task for an English major who didn't take a single math class at the University of Washington. Through persistence and hard work, she eventually became the highest performing math teacher in her district.

In 2009, the Arizona Department of Education decided that, as an intervention, the state would take over failing schools. The model was a modified version of receivership. Schools that were taken over by the state were required to remove their current principal and any instructional coaches on the campus. The state then placed a *Turnaround Principal* and two *Turnaround Coaches* to lead teaching and learning. The district could control virtually everything else – from finances to technology to facilities. Megan applied for and was selected as a *Turnaround Coach*, a two-year commitment. Although she could have been placed anywhere in the state, she was placed at a sister school in her current district.

After the two-year commitment, Megan transitioned to the district office where she worked as a staff developer. She helped mentor novice and struggling teachers as well as organized and facilitated district-wide professional development opportunities. Within a couple of years, she accepted a promotion to lead the district's Staff Development department.

While at the district office, she established a strong relationship with the then-superintendent. Each of the last two years Megan served in that department, her superintendent asked her to consider applying for a principalship. She respectfully declined the first year – the timing just wasn't right. However, her superintendent finally sat her down in the spring of 2015 and said, "This is the year, Megan." She applied, was selected, and has been the principal of Norma Jones School, a K-8 with nearly 550 students, for the past five years. You'll hear much more about her journey as we progress.

There are three recent events that led me to finally pen this book.

First, over the past four years, I have hired 17 new principals. Every year, I host a first-year principal meeting with two major goals. First, I simply like to break bread together and create a sense of community with them. There is so much fear, anxiety, and stress inherent in being a first-year principal that I like to force our new leaders to slow down enough to be reflective about their journey and intentional about their work. The first year is so critical to the long-term success of a principal. Second, I like to share with them the framework of this book - give them a specific roadmap on what matters (people), what doesn't matter (test scores), and what to avoid (going too fast, buying yourself new furniture, or traveling to Hawaii for a conference).

After one of these meetings, I remember coming home and saying to Megan, "I would have done anything to be a first-year principal in this district. Can you imagine having your boss tell you that your test scores and student achievement data in your first year doesn't matter, and that your ability to build relationships and establish trust and credibility with your people is what you'd be judged on? Sign me up!"

After this year's first-year principal meeting, one of our new principals said, "Although I am not sure what parts of this morning were most meaningful, because I think it all was, one thing is certain. My blood pressure has been cut in half. I am excited to get to work. A few hours ago I was scared and didn't know where to start. Now, I am ready."

This is reason one.

Periodically, I agree to give presentations as well as guest teach in various graduate courses around the valley. When asked to speak about K-12 leadership specifically, I always share the framework of this book. Time and time again, at the end of a talk (or via email exchanges the days following), I am asked if I have written or will write a book explaining the framework in more detail to serve as a guide for principals and school leaders to follow. I recently shared this framework with a group of aspiring and first-year school leaders and, once again, they asked me to write this book.

That's reason two.

The third reason is perhaps the most powerful. I used this BEFORE Teaching and Learning, or BTL, framework during my two principalships and experienced tremendous success. But, without a "first follower," this success could have simply been a byproduct of circumstance or leadership style, not the framework. While at Norma Jones School, Megan used BTL and has experienced, arguably, even more success than me. If this framework can work for two very different leaders in three very different settings spanning the entire K-12 continuum in three different districts, it can work for everyone looking to make transformative change.

That's reason three.

This is a practical book for practitioners. There are no untested leadership theories. This isn't educational philosophy or fiction. I do include research and several references to leadership books to provide background and context. The rest of the book is designed to help practitioners – all practitioners – do the work.

My hope and prayer is that this book can help superintendents and leadership directors better lead principals and assistant principals, especially new campus leaders, who struggle to plant roots and prepare for the marathon, not the sprint, of campus leadership.

This is also a book for first-year principals and assistant principals who so badly want to be successful, struggle with where to start, and know that, in most cases, the principals that once led the schools at which they taught could have done it so much better.

Finally, this is a book for seasoned principals and assistant principals who feel as though the climate and culture on their campuses isn't up to par and that they have to do something about it.

Regardless of who you are, what role you play, or how long you've been in the game, you must remember that there is so much work to be done BEFORE you worry about teaching and learning. This book is a great place to start.

Chapter 1
A Glimpse into Our Journeys

During my years as a principal, I was extremely fortunate to have led two amazing teams of dedicated educators – one at Carl T. Smith (CTS) Middle School and one at Camelback High School. Both schools reside within the city limits of Phoenix. With unwavering commitment to student and school transformation, these teams were able to create two very impressive success stories. Both schools experienced drastic increases in student achievement, improved state labels, and won awards.

In some ways, CTS and Camelback were very similar. They were both "majority minority" urban schools. Both had extremely high Free and Reduced Lunch rates - as high as 99%. Both had been plagued with drugs, gangs, violence, low student achievement, terrible morale, damaged culture, and a lack of vision. Both had struggling (and fantastic) teachers. Both had poorly behaved (and amazing) students.

In many other ways, however, the schools were completely different. One was a smaller middle school - approximately 400 students. The other was a large comprehensive high school - approximately 2,000 students. The middle school was geographically located near one of the most troubled intersections in Phoenix - poverty, prostitution, and gangs lingered day and night. The high school, conversely, was located near one of the wealthiest intersections in Arizona - big business, restaurants, and shopping. Students from impoverished neighborhoods south of the school rode public transportation to attend Camelback.

The middle school was new - only 3 years old. New schools lack tradition, history, and much of the politics that come with both. The high school was 60 years old. Older schools are wrought with crippling politics - generations of alumni, history, traditions, successes, failures, systems, beliefs, stories, and attitudes, to name a few. To say that turning around a newer, smaller school is an easier endeavor is an understatement. But to say that transforming any school is easy would be highly inaccurate. School transformation, regardless of the size, grade levels served, or the history of the school, is very complex and very challenging work.

Both schools that I led are great examples of this complexity. Here is a glimpse into how these journeys began.

Carl T. Smith Middle School

When the principal vacancy at CTS was posted in the spring of 2006, I did not intend to apply. In fact, I didn't at first. I was an assistant principal at JB Sutton Elementary - just wrapping up my second year out of the classroom. I was only 28. I had very recently been accepted into a doctoral program. Megan taught full time. Our daughter, our first child, was less than a year old. Being new parents while working full-time without family in town to assist was a major challenge. At the time, I was just not in a hurry to leave JB Sutton or the assistant principalship. I was comfortable. We were improving outcomes for students. I loved the staff, students, and community. I had a great principal and mentor, Mary Lou. I thought I was in the right place. And, on top of it all, I had now settled into the elementary school arena - CTS was a middle school. I wasn't ready for that. I didn't even want that.

I had visited CTS once earlier that year for a district technology meeting. I literally left thanking God that I didn't work there - that's a true story. The kids were out of control. The adults were miserable. The hallways were noisy. And the computer lab - at that time next to the cafeteria - didn't have thick enough walls to hide the chaos of the cafeteria at lunch.

CTS was built at one of the poorest and most dangerous intersections in Phoenix - gangs, prostitution, violence, and drugs plague that community - did then and still do today. Many in the school district at the time wondered if they should have even built a school in that neighborhood. It was often referred to as "the mistake." The vast majority of the students at CTS lived in extremely decrepit trailers. The poverty was staggering - 99% Free and Reduced Lunch rate. The only reason we didn't reach 100% is because we could never chase down all of the applications. Almost all qualified for free breakfast and lunch, not just reduced. If you know anything about the system, that's extreme poverty.

In 2006, only 11% of the 6th graders met the minimum standard on the state's mathematics assessment (meaning 89% didn't). Reading was not much better - around 25% met the standard. Unfortunately, student achievement was not just a 6th grade problem - the average percentage of students who met the minimum standard in all grade levels was somewhere between one quarter and one third. That meant that approximately 3 out of every 4 students were not proficient in reading or math - many of those not even close.

Not surprising, the climate, culture, and conditions of the campus were terrible. Even though the building was new, the issues ran deep.

It is for those reasons I didn't originally apply. It wasn't that I feared failure. I just didn't feel the call or the pull to take on such a huge task with my life in such great transition. But after some coaxing by the superintendent, some prayer, and lengthy conversations with Megan, I eventually applied and was given the job – not because I was qualified for the position but rather that I was literally only one of three people in the entire city who even submitted an application. Mind you, we are the fifth largest city in America.

I visited the campus three times that spring before I officially began. As you'll read about later, I believe it's critically important to learn and know as much as possible about the school you are leading before you begin to make any major decisions – hence, the three visits.

I vividly remember my first visit to CTS after being named principal in late spring. Much like an emergency room, the school operated under a constant state of triage. As a prime example, they had moved the ISS room to the principal's conference room in the front office so that the school secretary could double as the friendly face at the counter and the disciplinarian to the school's most disruptive and disrespectful students to her left. The In-School Suspension (ISS) monitor had quit. I didn't blame him. They couldn't find a replacement. I wasn't surprised.

You can imagine the image this portrayed to visitors like me. Ten study carols in the front office - tagging, etching, garbage, foul language, disruptions - and a secretary yelling at and threatening students who knew that there was no threat sufficient enough to merit a change in behavior.

That day, I met with the outgoing principal in her office. I asked her about the students and the teachers. Not surprisingly, I didn't get a very optimistic reaction.

She said, "You know, some good, some bad."

I asked if they would all be returning next year so that I could begin to focus on filling vacancies if needed. She said that there were a couple of ineffective teachers who may be resigning.

I asked when she would know. She quickly remarked, "Wait a minute. I'll go find out."

She left me in her office as she walked down to two teachers' classrooms to see if they planned to return. School was in session. I sat in her office for the time being. I could hear the secretary up front lecturing the ISS students. Lecturing is putting it nicely.

A teacher walked in looking for the principal. I introduced myself. She said that she was hopeful that they could "turn the ship around" but that it wouldn't be easy and it wouldn't be painless. She began to share horror stories just as the principal returned – teachers love to tell horror stories to new principals. The teacher quickly departed as the principal delivered bad news - the two ineffective teachers planned to stay.

I asked the principal for a copy of the bell schedule and a few other documents including the staff roster. I left her office. I then introduced myself to the office staff, stood in the hallway for a passing period, and hovered around the parking lot at dismissal. Not a pretty sight.

On my second visit that spring, I met with a group of teachers – a group that I was told was the "discipline committee" but later found out was just a group of disgruntled teachers who were fed up with the chaos. This is eerily similarly to Megan's story almost a decade later. I learned of fires in the bathroom, slashed teacher tires, urine and feces in the corners of the library and in the water fountains, fights and assaults in classrooms and in the hallways, food fights in the cafeteria, and extreme disrespect on a daily basis before, during, and after school. The principal was transitioning out, the teachers had given up, the students were in control. We didn't brainstorm any solutions at that point - I just wanted to learn more about the current state of student behavior and build some relationships.

I visited campus a third and final time right before school ended that spring. The staff had gotten together to create a list of recommendations for the new principal. There were twelve. The recommendations ranged from creating a block schedule to hiring a new elective teacher to creating a school-wide discipline program to needing a clock in the teacher workroom. I met with the entire staff, ran through the twelve recommendations, made no decisions that day other than installing a clock in the workroom during the meeting (a story I'll tell later), but wanted to let them know I valued their time, their effort, their recommendations, and them as educators and as people.

I remember leaving that day with mixed emotions. If a staff cared enough about the school to get together to generate and type twelve well-thought-out recommendations for the new principal, they couldn't be that bad. They also had a veteran, retired principal serving as the assistant principal who seemed to be a huge resource and turned out to be a mentor and dear friend. On the other hand, as I was leaving the campus early that morning, right at the beginning of the school day for the students, I saw unruly behavior, extreme tardiness, and no sense of urgency from staff or students.

It was painfully obvious why the vast majority of the students in the school failed to meet any sort of minimum academic standard.

Camelback High School

In the winter of 2009, during my third year as the principal at CTS, I was called to the superintendent's office for a meeting. I have to admit that I was nervous. On the surface, I had nothing to worry about from a performance perspective. CTS was now the top performing middle school in the district by all measures - state assessments, district benchmarks, and first place finishes at competitions like science fair, spelling bee, etc. The Governor visited our school to recognize our success. We won a very public award. However, I was told by the secretary that she didn't know why we were meeting. That's a bad sign.

That afternoon, I met with my boss. He began our conversation with, "So, what are your plans for next year?" Any time your boss asks that question, you know a job change is imminent. My boss proceeded to talk to me about another struggling middle school in the district that needed my leadership. He wanted me to take the same systems, same approach, same philosophy to that school the next school year.

I was heartbroken. We were on the verge of something amazing at CTS. Our growth was explosive – highest growth in the state of Arizona. The kids and staff were amazing. The parents had all bought in. But this wasn't a give-and-take conversation with room for compromise - the decision was final yet not public.

I remember doing two things that afternoon.

First, I took two of my most trusted teachers on a drive throughout the trailer parks to confidentially tell them about the meeting. I had to get it off my chest, and I had to start to worry about transition and sustainability of the vision, values, initiatives, performance.

The second thing I did was call my former boss. He was (and is) a friend and mentor. I wanted advice. I also wanted to let him know that I was considering the high school principalship he had asked me to consider the year before when he left our district. At the time he left the previous year, I remember telling him very clearly, "I will never become a high school principal. I love my wife and children too much to do that to them."

But, a year later, I figured that if I had to change schools that I might as well take on an even bigger challenge if Megan and the kids would approve. I began to study high schools "just in case." I submitted my application in the event they had any vacancies. At the time, they didn't.

A few weeks later, they posted two.

Before I knew it, I had made it to the third round of the interview process for the Camelback High School principalship. The first round was the paper screening. The second was an interview with the assistant superintendents. I obviously did well enough to get by but literally knew nothing about high schools other than my personal experience with them as a student, the few books I had read recently, and the day I spent shadowing a friend of mine. I felt under-prepared to say the least.

The third round was a "community forum" in the choir room at Camelback. When I pulled into the parking lot it was packed. I remember thinking to myself as I walked into the building, "Wow. For a school that is rumored to be in a state of complete apathy, I can't believe how many parents and community members are here." But when I walked in, the room was nearly empty. The cars in the parking lot, you may ask? A facility rental in the auditorium. As for the choir room, just 30-40 showed up to ask questions and render their vote. Megan and the kids were among the group.

There were three finalists, and we all had to answer questions generated by those in attendance. Everyone - the students, parents, teachers, and district personnel who had actually shown up - seemed intimidating. Had I known then what I know now, they should have been much more welcoming. After all, they were lucky that anyone wanted to be the principal of that school in its then-current condition.

The candidates introduced themselves as a group, were ushered into a waiting area, and called back out to the floor one-by-one. The questions were very telling - questions about losing all of the white kids and wanting them back, about a lack of leadership, a lack of vision, a lack of teamwork, a damaged faculty and staff, and a struggling student population.

The conversations with the community members before the meeting, the questions and reactions to those questions during the forum, and the "meetings after the meeting" all painted a picture of a poisonous environment that led to the downfall of a once great educational institution.

After the forum, my name was forwarded to the superintendent for the fourth and final round. In that meeting, the superintendent continued to tell the story of a very damaged place. He said that teachers picketed the previous principal before school just outside of the parking lot. He showed data that Camelback was then tied for the lowest achieving high school in the district. He shared examples of emails that he had gotten from faculty and staff about the condition of the school in terms of climate, culture, performance, staff and student behavior. I did not leave that meeting inspired.

Camelback had once been one of the highest performing public schools in Arizona. Nestled near the foothills of a beautiful city-center mountain and in the backyard of an intersection bustling with businesses and high-rise condos, Camelback was once home to the sons and daughters of the most wealthy, prominent, and educated Phoenicians.

From the mid-1950's to the mid-1980's, Camelback thrived academically and athletically. Then, desegregation hit in the mid-1980's. The boundaries of Camelback shifted. The population changed drastically. White flight struck the school. The school - its beliefs, its systems, its people - didn't evolve to meet the needs of the changing demographic. The results were terrible. A very dark 25 years ensued - gangs, drugs, violence, high dropout rates, low graduation rates, declining enrollment, declining sports and arts programs (such as a band with 13 students), declining achievement, and extreme principal turnover plagued the school.

When I arrived at Camelback High School in 2009, I was my secretary's 11th principal in 15 years. Veterans on staff say that I was the 15th in 20 years. Faculty told stories about a shooting after school that resulted in a bloody body being dragged into the principal's office where they waited for an ambulance. The student survived. I listened to story after story about fights, riots (whether they actually were or not), gang activity, academic apathy, the downfall of a generation. I heard messages of despair. The school lacked pride, it lacked hope.

When I asked my new secretary who the most respected and wise teacher on campus was, and if I could trust her to tell it to me straight, she arranged a meeting. The next day, I met with the teacher. I asked her what she would do if she was the principal. I asked her simply, "Where do I start?"

She said, "Just help us heal."

Norma Jones Elementary School

Norma Jones, formerly Rose Heights Elementary School (a story you'll hear about in a moment), is located in a community much like Carl T. Smith. It suffers from generational poverty – the school's Free and Reduced Lunch rate is 95%. The campus itself had not seen many quality upgrades or improvements over its 50 years, other than a new gymnasium. It did not have adequate fencing or gates to ensure security, and its current paint job, courtesy of a community service endeavor, was a poorly-done mix of yellow, blue, beige, and neon green. It had no windows for safety reasons. Student achievement had continued to decline, with the school receiving a C- letter grade (2 points from a D) from the Arizona Department of Education. There were no school-wide expectations or systems for student behavior.

It was Board meeting night in Roosevelt, the night when Megan was to be approved to serve as the new principal at Rose Heights Elementary School. The superintendent was thrilled for her and had called her earlier in the week to congratulate her again. Megan was excited but very nervous.

About two hours before the Board meeting, her superintendent called. There was trouble.

The outgoing principal had been at the school for nearly 30 years. She was beloved. She had spent the last 10 years as the principal and the previous 15-20 years as a teacher there. The community – both internal and external – assumed that the current assistant principal would become the next principal.

But, obviously, that was not going to be the case.

Unbeknownst to Megan, the outgoing principal and a few others had been rallying the troops (mainly parents) to stage a protest at the Board meeting. It also happened to be the night that the outgoing principal would be recognized for her retirement.

Megan and I decided that, as difficult as it would be, we should attend. If it fell apart and she was not approved, it would be good to know the who, the what, and the why. Likewise, if she was approved, it would also be good to know the who, what, and why. We made the drive down to South Phoenix that evening. Neither of us were looking forward to it. I remember telling her, "Put on your thick skin and remember they don't know you. So whatever they say, don't let it bother you. They've been coached to say horrible things about you."

Sure enough, there was quite the crowd at the meeting. Some were there in support of Megan but didn't speak publicly. There were other teachers and staff there in opposition but they didn't speak either. Those who spoke at the *Call to the Public* were mainly parents and community members. The common message they shared was that they wanted the assistant principal to be the principal and that they didn't believe they had a voice in the selection process of the new principal. Near the end of the *Call to the Public,* in one of those rare moments of silence, a 4th or 5th grader in the audience turned to his mom and said loudly enough for most in the room to hear, "But what if she's actually really good, mom?"

The Board voted unanimously to approve Megan as the new principal at Rose Heights. Unfortunately for Megan, things only got worse from there.

To begin the relationship building process, she asked the outgoing principal if she could meet with her leadership team before everyone vanished for the summer. The principal arranged for a meeting. Megan was very excited to meet the new team, learn more about the school, and begin to identify some potential starting points. However, when Megan arrived, it became very apparent that the group of teachers the principal asked to attend this meeting were not, in fact, the leadership team but rather anyone willing to show up. It was not a productive meeting. The outgoing principal dominated the meeting and didn't allow Megan to speak much at all. Immediately after the meeting, Megan assumed she and the principal would be able to sit down and talk. However, the outgoing principal went right into her office with a few teachers and closed the door.

It got worse.

A couple of weeks later, we were on our family vacation in June – we always take a family summer vacation no matter how crazy our lives get. Megan's phone rang. It was a district office number. Megan answered. The conversation went something like this:

> "Hello, Megan, this is Mrs. Jackson, the Title I Director. I am just calling to see how you want to handle a major issue at your new school. I am in receipt of a stack of timesheets for most of the Rose Heights staff to work over the summer. It's mainly for 'curriculum writing' although it's pretty vague what they'll actually be working on. They are signed and approved by the outgoing principal. The problem is, it's a massive amount of hours – an unusually excessive amount of hours – and will completely deplete your entire Title I budget. If you approve, you won't have any Title I funds until November or December of next year. You

won't be able to offer any leadership retreats, professional development, or student tutoring for about six months."

"Well, what are my options?" Megan asked.

"If you'd like me to deny the requisitions I will. It's your school now," she answered. "Or, if you are worried that denying them will create even more bad will at Rose Heights, I am happy to approve them. It's your call."

Megan decided to not get involved and let the requisitions get approved as written. Denying summer pay for over half her new staff could have been absolutely disastrous, politically speaking, even though having no Title funds for half a year wasn't a walk in the park either.

It got worse.

Before she knew it, it was the evening before her first official day with her new staff. Megan had decided to give them an entire day in their classrooms to get settled before hosting the welcome back staff meeting, which was scheduled for the second day. She knew that teachers want to be in their classrooms as much as possible that first week back. As for the first staff meeting, Megan had worked all summer to make sure it was perfect. It was set to be a great balance of humor and humility, purpose and planning, and team-building and training.

The first day got off to a great start. There was good energy on campus. Teachers were in and out of the office, setting up bulletin boards, and getting supplies. It felt very normal. Megan was feeling more optimistic about the start of school.

However, the next morning – the morning of the first all-staff meeting – the school clerk came into the office absolutely distraught. "What? What is it?" she asked.

"It's Ms. Jones," she responded. She's in the hospital and they don't think she'll make it!"

The previous evening, the former principal had been on a walk with her partner and dogs when she fell, most likely from a stroke or aneurism, and hit her head. She was in the hospital on life-support.

So, Megan gathered herself, made an "all call," and asked all faculty and staff to meet in the library for an emergency meeting. It was not exactly what she had envisioned for her first faculty meeting. She went on to announce that their beloved principal was in ICU and that the prognosis wasn't good. The emotions ran high. Some people went home. Some got back to work. Some went to the hospital.

Megan cancelled the planned meeting for the day and allowed staff to do whatever they needed to do. Megan did her best to continue preparations for the school year that was starting in less than a week. She met with her superintendent to discuss how to handle the week. Questions swirled in Megan's head regarding how to still start the year strong, communicate logistics, schedules, and even team-build with her new staff. How would she respect the emotions during this tragic time while also ensuring that the 550 students would get a good start to their school year? At the same time, some staff began to complain about other staff members taking advantage of the situation to not be at work getting ready for the year.

It got worse.

That Thursday, right after the district convocation ceremony where they did a moment of silence for Ms. Jones, she passed away – three hours before the planned Meet the Teacher Night. While much of the community was aware of the situation, many were not. Megan's first introduction to the students and families of the school essentially went like this: "Hi, I'm your new principal, Megan Gestson. I have some tragic news… a few hours ago, your beloved former principal passed away."

Megan's first week with students involved coordinating social workers for grieving students and helping staff to organize the memorial service held during that first week. Almost immediately, talk began to circulate regarding renaming either the new gym or the entire school after the former principal. Board members with conflicting opinions showed up on her campus (the first and only time in her first four years as principal) to discuss what should be renamed. Megan was asked to spend time collecting input from students and families on what to rename, if anything. Ultimately, the board voted to rename the school. All of this was within the first month of school.

Needless to say, Megan's start as a school leader was far from what she had planned for or envisioned. She knew the school was in desperate need of improvement, and she had a clear plan ready in terms of steps to begin that process. But much of that plan was interrupted by the tragedy. Systems and structures that were originally going to be put in place prior to school starting were delayed for months. However, sticking to the BTL framework, she continued to build relationships and learn about the school, the community, and the history – all of which helped her to successfully move forward and make change when the timing was right.

Carl T. Smith, Camelback, and Jones are different in many ways, from grade levels served to zip code. But they are also very similar – they were underperforming, dysfunctional, and obviously lacked the systems and structures necessary to drive positive outcomes for staff and students alike. I begin with these stories to show how challenging this work truly can be and to demonstrate that, even in the most dreadful of circumstances, thoughtful, intentional, and strategic leadership can yield amazing results as you'll see throughout the remainder of this book. The key to successful reform, in many ways, is to get off to the right start – or, better yet, to avoid a bad one.

Chapter 2
Where Not to Start

The Camelback teacher I met with that day was truly wise. When I asked her where I should start, she didn't talk about student achievement. She didn't reference benchmark assessments, PLC's, or lesson plans. She didn't recommend stronger curriculum or more accountability for teachers. She simply said, "Just help us heal."

The question, "Where do I start?" is probably the most common I hear today from new and struggling school leaders. We will spend much of this book examining that very question.

For many reasons that I'll explore shortly, there is a predominant school reform model used all throughout education today – in elementary schools, middle schools, high schools, district schools, charter schools, and private schools alike. I believe that this model – what I call the Test Score First, or TSF, model - is extremely harmful to school leaders, teachers, students, school performance, and even the system in general. The TSF model is a model that, in many ways, disrespects educators, ignores research, and is making school leadership less and less desirable and doable. And, quite candidly, it doesn't work.

Let's first talk about why this model isn't effective and how it's harming education today.

In the Test Score First model, while pursuing immediate increases in student achievement, personal relationships, job satisfaction, employee retention, long-term sustainability of student results, and even personal health and wellness do not matter. By succumbing to the intense pressure that comes with being a school leader in the post-NCLB era, TSF principals ignore everything that change theorists and human psychologists tell us about motivation, relationships, school reform, and organizational transformation. At the end of the day, all that matters in this current accountability-obsessed environment is test scores and state labels.

So, unfortunately, most new principals – often because that's all they've been taught or told to do – focus on teaching, learning, and testing from day one and fight the good fight like everyone else.

In the TSF model, school leaders show little to no concern for their people. They do not take time to build relationships with teachers, staff, or even the community. They do not pause to learn about the history of the school or learn what matters most to the staff, the students, and the parents. Very foolishly, TSF leaders don't even find out what initiatives have been implemented in the past and, subsequently, failed or succeeded.

Furthermore, TSF principals don't find or make time to engage positively and intentionally with students. They ignore issues and problems on campus and in the community that, although they may not have a direct impact on student achievement, do negatively affect the working climate for adults and learning environment for students. On top of it all, principals don't typically create systems and structures for teachers and other stakeholders to engage in the decision-making process that drives teaching and learning on campus. School improvement initiatives are often top-down, are focused on teacher accountability, and are not sustainable over time.

Yet, despite these obvious issues, and others, this approach still happens every day in education across this country. TSF principals view test scores and assessment data as the means, the ends, and everything in between. If student achievement data is trending in the right direction, no matter the bloodshed, the grind continues.

I believe we are nearing a crisis in school leadership - if we aren't already there. And when you step back and examine the absurdity of the predominant model - the TSF model – it becomes painfully obvious that this approach isn't effective.

In order to clearly illustrate what the TSF model looks like and feels like, let's take a moment to examine a typical, yet hypothetical, school reform effort.

Rockefeller School

A new principal is hired at Rockefeller. The new principal does no analysis of the climate, culture, systems, and structures of the school. Instead, the principal immediately concentrates on improving test scores with a laser-like focus on curriculum, instruction, and assessment.

Professional development for teachers is one of the first major initiatives - after all, teachers must be the problem. Rigor for students is increased. Instructional initiatives are launched for teachers. Assessments at the grade level and/or content level are aligned. The principal steadily begins to apply more pressure on teachers to get their kids to perform better (and faster). As a result, teachers test kids almost as much as they teach them and meet often to review performance data.

Pressure continues to increase throughout the year during data chats. Kids get grouped strategically for interventions, re-teach sessions, and, in some schools, enrichment. In most cases, kids on the "bubble" are targeted in order to immediately increase the percentage of students who pass assessments - school, district, and state. This cycle and pressure continues all year, typically during teacher prep periods.

At the end of the year, test scores are released. Scores increase. The school's label improves.

The principal is praised and feels accomplished, though exhausted. The superintendent recognizes the principal at a board meeting. An article is written in the district's quarterly newsletter about the school's improvement. The principal is motivated to continue.

Pressure on teachers to perform increases. The teaching staff is miserable – overworked, stressed, and under-appreciated. They are not motivated to continue. They cannot keep pace physically, emotionally, or professionally for much longer. Burnout for new and veteran teachers is palpable. Regardless, the principal puts summer cadres together to plan curriculum, assessment, and instructional improvements for the following year to get even "better."

In the fall, the work load for teachers gets heavier. More paperwork. More benchmark exams. More formative assessments. More data. Teams meet more often. Prep periods are almost completely lost. Good and bad teachers alike consider leaving; many ultimately do. Kids lose recess and special area classes (in elementary & middle school) and electives (in high school). Test scores continue to climb modestly. The principal is not content with growth - a lecture during PLC's and at a staff meeting leaves staff feeling even less motivated, more frustrated, and terribly undervalued.

Kids are not taught to truly think critically at Rockefeller. There are no more field trips or genuine learning experiences. There is no focus on character education. Students aren't developed to become future leaders and problem-solvers. Elementary school students read about recess in a history book. However, students have learned how to pass an exam because of strategic and targeted interventions aligned to assessments.

"This must really be working." The principal wins another award. Morale continues to plummet. A new year begins. More pressure. Repeat.

In thousands of schools and districts today, this scenario is reality. Too many educators know this all too well. In fact, if you are an aspiring principal who happens to still be in a classroom, you are either laughing hysterically or hyperventilating because of how accurate this scenario is – it doesn't matter the grade level, school, district, or state, this is education today.

You may ask why this model even exists. I argue that it's still the primary model for four reasons.

First, to the outside world, or at least on the surface, it seems to work. Schools earn A+ awards, A and B state labels, and are considered "Excelling" or "Exemplary" when they increase scores. And the quicker the better! Go from a D to an A in your state's labeling system, and you'll be on the front page of your local newspaper with a plaque in your hand surrounded by students whom you haven't met because you spend most of your time in your conference room analyzing data and pressuring teachers.

Second, as aforementioned, there is such intense pressure to perform immediately. The Every Student Succeeds Act, or ESSA (previously NCLB), state accountability systems, the school choice movement, and district and parent expectations influence decision-making. This has created a culture in education that all but forces school leaders to pursue academic improvement instantly. Local newspapers, national magazines, and educational journals track and publish each school's status and state accountability label, in most states now a letter grade. Educators feel crippling pressure to avoid a bad grade. Superintendents, principals, and teachers feel as though their jobs hinge upon immediate performance. Parents pay attention to it. Enrollment, money, reputation depend on it.

The third reason is simply that we believe that if we are truly in this business "for the kids," it seems harmful and contradictory not to start immediately with improving learning.

The fourth and final reason is that we really do not know any other way - or at least we have forgotten or don't have or make time for it. Consulting firms now make millions adhering to the TSF model. Trainings, summer conferences, and district professional development support this approach. Time and time again, we are told that rigorous curriculum, aligned assessments, strong intervention systems and re-teach sessions, and improved pedagogy (a focus on differentiated instruction and student engagement) will lead to better test scores. (And they do by the way. But in what order and at what sacrifice?)

To make matters even worse, principals today are now taught (or at least learn how) to play the system. Our country, and every state within it, has a system for labeling schools. Often, states use a combination of student growth and student proficiency on a state-sponsored exam to label schools. Like in most systems, there are shortcuts. Principals learn how to target "bubble" students, provide interventions for "bottom quartile" students, and determine which web-based programs are most effective in getting students to pass the state exam. In many cases today, we are merely spiking test scores to get favorable accountability labels.

We are completely wrong. Students and teachers and school leaders are losing.

In order to further demonstrate the absurdity of this approach, I want to share yet another scenario. This time, the scenario has nothing to do with education. Instead, it involves something we all know and love – food.

Trendy Bar and Grill

Imagine for a moment that a TSF principal has just been named the manager of a once-popular restaurant, Trendy Bar and Grill.

Trendy has been experiencing high employee turnover for the past 5 years. The principal is the third manager in that time. Quarterly profits have been declining for the last eight quarters. Customer satisfaction is at an all-time low. Rumor on the street is that, if the principal can't change the trajectory at Trendy, the restaurant will have to close its doors.

The principal stops by for a visit a few days before she takes the reigns. The climate at Trendy is terrible. Employees do not get along. Keeping good employees on staff is obviously difficult to do - one quit right there on the spot. The quality of the staff is less than impressive, or at least that's the impression on the surface.

Despite its name, nothing about Trendy is trendy. The colors are old and stale. The front of the restaurant looks shabby. The bathrooms haven't been remodeled in years. The food has become mediocre. Because of the toxic working environment, customer service is terrible. Unhappy employees can't create happy environments for customers. Toxicity breeds toxicity.

Perhaps worst of all is Trendy's Yelp rating. It is now below three stars. The local newspaper just wrote an article about the doomed future of Trendy.

It's Monday, the first day on the job. The TSF principal arrives and begins her work.

There is no initial discussion about actually improving the product or the process - just the Yelp scores and the articles written about Trendy in the paper.

The principal creates a plan to get the 3-star rating to a 4-star rating - and as quickly as possible. This includes having family members and employees log on to Yelp to submit 4's and 5's to spike the ratings. To "sweeten" the deal, Trendy starts to offer a free dessert to anyone who submits a 5-star rating on Yelp while at the table.

Next, the principal provides intensive training for the servers on how to be better servers. This training is done by an outside organization that specializes in professional development for servers. Even though there are 20 on staff, all with varying levels of experience and expertise, all employees attend the same training. Servers at Trendy become highly offended because they all have different backgrounds, do not want someone from the outside telling them what to do, and don't think they are the problem. They blame the chef.

The principal then sends the chef to a conference in a sunny region of the United States to attend a chef's institute. He comes back a week later with a sun tan, a few new ideas, and a list of products that he wants the restaurant to purchase.

The chef also says that he has spoken with other chefs from across the country, and that he is now convinced that the problem at Trendy is the servers. Their attitude and customer service taints the customers' experience so much so that they rate the food (and, therefore, the restaurant) terribly.

Frustration mounts inside of Trendy. The break room, bathroom, and parking lot after work are dangerous places to be. Employee turnover and attendance worsens.

An article is written in the newspaper about Trendy's new 4-star Yelp rating. The new manager is interviewed on the Sunday morning news because of the drastic improvement. A plaque is hung on the wall. Morale hits an all-time low.

Welcome to education in the 21st Century.

Chapter 3
Where to Start

Obviously, we know there is a much better way to approach school (and restaurant) reform. The TSF model is not sustainable. It's also not genuine. For those of us who are intimately involved in educational leadership, we know how dire the current situation is. Teachers are becoming burned out - even the best and brightest and most eager and energetic are talking about leaving. Many already have.

Principal tenure continues to fall way short of ideal. One quarter of all schools have a principal vacancy each year, and half of all principals leave by their third year. New standards and measurements are on the horizon - new pressure, new evaluation systems, new pay for performance structures. With so much "new," we can't continue to operate within an "old" leadership paradigm.

Nearly a decade ago, I became intrigued with companies like Microsoft, Google, and Southwest that focused on creating and sustaining amazing working environments for their employees. I knew, as a novice school principal, I had to do more for my faculty and staff, not just my student body. What I learned from the business sector changed my educational leadership journey forever.

It was very clear that in the business sector, the mission, vision, and values of these organizations were known, shared, developed, and displayed by all. Employee loyalty and retention far exceeded industry standards at these high-performing, employee-centered companies.

They knew that strong working environments ripened the soil for innovation, creativity, and happiness. Happy employees work longer, work harder, and produce more. After all, companies like Google surely don't put pool tables in their offices and offer Friday happy hours to reduce productivity, stifle innovation, harm employee retention, and diminish quarterly profits.

Southwest Airlines knows this well. The happier their employees, the happier their customers. Satisfied customers are repeat customers. The better their working environment, the better the profit. Today, they are the most profitable airline of all time.

Using what the business sector already knows, what the research says about human psychology and motivation, and our experiences over the past decade in school leadership, we will begin to explore a much different approach to school leadership. I call it BEFORE Teaching and Learning, or BTL, because it describes six components, or steps, a new leader should take *before* beginning an intense focus on teaching and learning.

Even though the improvement of teaching and learning is the ultimate goal of schooling today, that doesn't mean we must start there. In fact, I maintain in this book that we absolutely shouldn't. Simply put, there is a tremendous amount of work that must be done *before* we even begin to address what is known by educators as *T&L*.

I am, by no means, minimizing the importance of improving teaching and learning. This is our business. We are judged by it. We are paid to improve it. Parents and the media care about it. Just as an entrepreneur can't say that quarterly profits don't matter, educational leaders can't ignore student achievement. However, how and when a school leader starts to really address achievement is at the heart of this book.

I will describe the model in detail in the next chapter. For now, I want to spend some time sharing a 30,000-foot view of the look and feel of the BTL framework. In order to do so, we will revisit our two hypothetical scenarios, but this time from a much different lens - the BTL lens. We'll start back at Rockefeller.

Rockefeller School

As in the previous scenario – a new principal is hired at Rockefeller. As is always the case, the expectation is to increase student achievement on district, state, and national exams as soon as possible.

The principal understands and respects this reality yet intentionally defers an intense focus on teaching and learning improvement and begins to do some relationship building and information seeking first. She meets with teachers and classified staff to learn about them as people as well as gain any insight into issues on campus such as parking, supplies, copy machines, duties, the staff lounge, lesson plans, and scheduling. The principal finds solutions to many of these problems, in some instances with the help of time-bound (ad hoc) subcommittees, and fixes them swiftly.

She then meets with parents, learns about challenges in the community with crosswalks and buses, and on the campus with lunchtime supervision. The principal changes the lunch duty schedule and re-routes the main crosswalk. She meets with the district to adjust the bus schedule.

The principal meets with student groups, listens to issues with supplies, technology, passing periods, bathrooms, and ketchup in the cafeteria. She buys new ketchup dispensers for the cafeteria, installs mirrors and tampon dispensers in the bathrooms, and increases the passing period by one minute but then tightens up on the tardy policy.

She then decides she needs to get a little "tough on crime," so to speak. Using focus groups of students, parents, and staff to provide ongoing input, she creates very clear behavioral expectations for all students and strategically tackles the behaviors of a few key students who seem to have set the tone on campus - sometimes a few informal student leaders can drive school culture more than the principal. These behaviors also hinder the learning environment for so many others.

Addressing the behaviors of these students sends a strong message to staff, students, and parents and sets a tone of behavioral and academic excellence on campus. A safe and orderly campus is paramount to school and student excellence.

The principal gains almost-instant credibility and momentum. The staff begins to trust the new principal who obviously means business, seeks input, and listens to, respects, and acts upon suggestions from all stakeholder groups.

The principal forms a community network - a group of engaged, dedicated external individuals willing to problem solve, fundraise, and support change. She recognizes that school reform takes time, talent, and treasures not often found within the school alone. She also starts a Parent Advisory Council to ensure parents' voices are always represented.

Random staff celebrations keep the ball rolling. Staff being viewed as the solution, not the problem, ripens the soil for explosive improvement. The new couches and coffee maker in the staff lounge are not a bad addition either.

The principal then forms two leadership teams – one to address academic culture and systems and another to address organizational culture and systems. The teams spend months identifying issues on campus (in and out of the classroom) and researching best practices around the country. They do site visits to local *reputationally* exemplary schools.

The various teams eventually develop a new mission, vision, and initiatives to be implemented next year, not immediately, that fit the specific needs, interests, and capacity of the school and community. Teams continue to plan throughout the year to set the stage for the next year, not this year.

More random ice cream parties and bagel breakfasts occur. The year is almost over. Test scores are released. Scores are relatively stagnant. The principal is tired, slightly disappointed, but anticipated such scores. The teachers and community are energized, excited, and optimistic for and about the change despite not seeing an initial spike in test scores.

The principal doesn't receive any public awards but the staff throws her a "Thank You" party for respecting them and believing in them.

Summer cadres finalize systems and structure changes and prepare for implementation. The new school year begins. New systems and structures are launched. Teams monitor progress and adjust accordingly. The psychological climate of the campus is also monitored by the principal; she adjusts timelines accordingly - speeding up in some areas, slowing down in others. The principal cancels meetings and sends teachers home early to show her appreciation for their hard work.

The staff does a community service project together in the community. A strong sense of team/family is growing. Test scores are released. Scores improve. The staff celebrates (again).

Summer break of Year 2 arrives. Cadres continue the momentum to seamlessly launch another year. Day 1, Week 1, Month 1 go off without a hitch. Now that the systems and structure changes are successfully implemented and staff has adjusted, the campus begins to focus on real performance – teaching and learning, not test scores. Teaching gets stronger, learning improves. Kids are the focus, not the state exam.

The staff organizes and pulls off a flash mob at dismissal on a Friday to surprise the kids. Staff morale continues to improve; student motivation increases. The synergy is tangible. Test scores are released. Scores significantly improve. An award. A party. A new year begins. Repeat.

This is obviously a stark contrast to the TSF model where people don't matter, but rather numbers and immediate performance do. In the BTL model, people matter, climate and culture matter, systems and structures matter, sustainability matters. As you can see, performance matters, achievement matters, state accountability labels also matter. But they don't matter more than people. And they don't matter right away.

Depending on your experience in education, this may seem a bit "far-fetched," especially in the current reality of education today. Believe me, I get it. Megan lives it every day as a principal. I now lead a system of 21 schools, 3,100 employees, and 28,000 students where I must grapple with the same politics, pressure, and performance insanity as the rest of the country.

But what I can tell you is this - the above Rockefeller School scenario, the next iteration of the Trendy Bar and Grill scenario we'll revisit in a moment, and the remainder of this book are not based on theories and hypothesis. Both Megan and I, with three separate school communities, were able to do this. It takes focus, intentionality, and clarity. It takes boldness and confidence. It takes a strong team. It takes time. But it has been done. And it can be done in your school or across your school system.

Let's now take a brief moment to revisit the Trendy Bar and Grill scenario in order to dig a little deeper into the BTL framework before describing it explicitly. You'll see a similar approach to people, relationships, planning, and reform.

Trendy Bar and Grill

Even though quarterly profits are the end game, a real business reformer knows that change takes time. He determines other key indicators outside of quarterly profits, such as staff turnover and the number of first-time and repeat customers, by which to measure initial progress.

The new manager knows that he must know his people and the problems in the organization before creating any sweeping changes. He first spends time getting to know his employees and customers. He meets with servers and chefs separately.

He surveys and interviews customers. He builds as much background knowledge as possible to be better informed in the future.

In those conversations and surveys, he learns that the image of the restaurant, at least initially, is one of the biggest issues. Soon thereafter, after seeking input from the team, he has the restaurant painted. He then has the bathrooms remodeled. He upgrades the landscaping and entry of the restaurant. The website also gets a major facelift.

The manager then adds a couple new items to the menu using the expertise of the chef and input from the servers about what they hear from customers. They have new, shiny menus printed. He improves the *happy hour* deals to generate more business, not necessarily more profit.

He opens the restaurant later than usual one day per month to allow for team-building, which includes creating a shared mission and vision.

Teams of servers and chefs visit highly profitable restaurants in the area. They host innovation sessions where employees, not the manager, make suggestions for improvements - the manager's job is simply to say yes to the good ideas. The servers and the chefs implement new ideas - new menus, new products, new services. The team grows closer - they actually become a team.

Six months later, Trendy is trendy again. The previous 3-star rating is now well over four (without spiking), and the reform effort is sustainable and synergistic.

Through a focus on relationships, culture, collaboration, problem-solving, and true transformation, these two teams - both Rockefeller and Trendy - were able to drive performance and effectiveness. Best of all, by using the BTL framework, they were able to do so without sacrificing job satisfaction or work climate. In fact, quite the contrary - work climate and collaborative structures in many ways contributed to better performance. Best of all, these teams were also able to create changes that will be steady and sustainable for years to come.

Chapter 4
BEFORE Teaching and Learning

The BEFORE Teaching and Learning framework is designed to be simple and practical. Although it's based on research and study, you'll see that it has been developed through the lens of a school leader looking for practical ways to launch school reform. BTL has six clearly defined components - components that are not necessary designed to take place in a perfect 1-6 order, as they are often intertwined and iterative. However, the model is fairly linear with most components naturally falling into place before others. Here is a high-level look at the model:

B: Build Relationships - develop genuine personal and professional relationships with individuals and teams of individuals on campus and in the community

E: Enhance Your Institutional Knowledge - understand the history, relationships, power structures, systems, points of pride, areas of frustration, and dreams and aspirations of a wide variety of stakeholders

F: Fix the Fixables (Don't Create Change) - find solutions to simple, surface-level problems that improve working and learning conditions as well as build the momentum and credibility necessary for real change (later)

O: Organize Leadership, Learning, and Listening Structures - establish teams and structures that enhance inclusivity and collaboration to broaden voice and perspective as well as increase motivation and empowerment

R: Review, Research, Reflect, Redesign - allocate time

and space for individuals and teams to reflect upon the current performance level(s) of the school as well as study successful schools, school models, and people to drive future vision, mission, goals, and initiatives

E: Engage, Excite, and Establish Expectations for Your Students - focus on improving pride, engagement, behaviors, and beliefs among students to expedite the improvement process

There are a few important things to note about the model as we move forward.

First, as mentioned above, although the model is not meant to go in an exact order, some components do fit well sequentially. You should build relationships before rewriting a mission statement. You should learn about issues at lunchtime before you change the lunch schedule. You should seek input from teachers and the front office staff before changing how teachers get supplies. In other words, you shouldn't start fixing problems on your campus until you have built some relationships, know what the problems actually are, and determine how you can best solve them based on observations and the feedback of others.

Second, you'll notice that some components can be done simultaneously. For example, as you intentionally *Build Relationships* with your staff, you should also intentionally *Enhance Your Institutional Knowledge* by learning more about the school, the community, the history.

However, be careful. Relationship building is relationship building. If during a relationship-building coffee meeting with the English Department Chair you are asking more questions like, "What's your opinion on why the previous administration abandoned the reading curriculum" versus "Tell me more about your kids" or "What else did you do on your road trip this summer," then you have forgotten the point of "B," and the E, F, O, R, or E won't even matter later in your tenure. Relationships are authentic and developed over time through respect and consistency. People know if you are being genuine. They pay attention as to whether or not you practice what you preach.

The third thing you'll notice - and this extremely important – is that although I'll give you very clear examples and suggestions, BTL is not a "box checking" tool or model. You are not done with *Build Relationships*, for example, after a few coffee meetings with a few key stakeholders. If you ever catch yourself saying something like, "Well, I've had coffee with six people, lunch with my custodians, and a dinner meeting with my office staff. Now I can move on to enhancing my institutional knowledge," then you've lost sight of the purpose and power of this model.

Likewise, to really drive this point home, you can't check the box and claim victory on *Engage, Excite, and Establish Expectations for Students* after a couple successful assemblies - this work is ongoing. Student relationships, student voice, and student conduct (attitudes, behaviors, beliefs) must be a school-wide and staff-wide commitment every week, every quarter, every year.

Again, not a box-checking tool.

Finally, there is nothing in the model about test scores or student achievement. There is nothing in the model about data or word walls. There is nothing in the model about Professional Learning Communities, "House" systems or "Advisory" in middle schools or high schools, or leveled reading programs in elementary schools. You won't even read about Common Formative Assessments, benchmarking, interventions, coaching, or professional development.

But I mention all of these now (PLCs, CFAs, etc.) for two reasons.

The first reason is that these really do matter - they just can't be the focus right away. What's great about this day and age in education is that we have access to the latest and greatest practices and examples of how to improve teaching and learning right at our fingertips (or a plane ride to a conference). We know that PLCs, for example, when done correctly, can have a huge impact on teaching and learning outcomes. We know that creating smaller, more personalized learning settings for students improves relationships and achievement. We know that the creation of CFAs help teacher teams and students get real-time feedback that drive learning in targeted areas. Again, these are important - they just aren't first in the BTL framework.

Which leads us to the second reason we mentioned these areas - they (best practices in education today) have to become the focus at some point. The idea of "**BEFORE** Teaching and Learning" is based on the understanding that, at some point, there must be a focus **on** teaching and learning.

This doesn't mean that you ever stop fixing problems, building relationships, or engaging students. But it does mean that school communities have limited bandwidth and should only tackle a few key initiatives a time. At some point, once culture, climate, systems, and resources are nicely aligned, your teams need to focus **on** teaching and learning to drive real outcomes. After all, improving practice and performance, as Richard Elmore once wrote, is the ultimate goal of school reform. Just do it at the right time and at the right pace.

So, in summary, before we move on:

Step 1: **BEFORE** Teaching and Learning (this book)
Step 2: **On** Teaching and Learning (not this book but very important later when your school community is ready)

Also, other than the brief mention of it in the following paragraph, it is important to note that at no point will I formally suggest when the **before** is over and the **on** teaching and learning officially begins. This is up to each individual principal and his or her team. School environments – the culture, climate, systems, structures, politics, achievement –

vary so greatly that only school communities can determine when it's time to shift the focus.

What I can tell you from our experiences is this. In Megan's case, it was the third year that her school became hyper-focused on teaching and learning. At my middle school, we became really serious about *T&L* in year two. At my high school, believe it or not, it wasn't until year five that we made the shift. That wasn't my original goal, but, simply put, it took a few years to clean up a few decades of issues. Despite these 2, 3, and 5-year timelines, all three schools did show tremendous growth and achievement **before** the more intense focus **on** teaching and learning. These improvements were simply a by-product of larger improvements to climate, culture, and systems.

Here is a glimpse into the growth that all three schools experienced using the *BEFORE Teaching and Learning* model. Keep in mind, most of this growth took place **before** an intensive focus **on** teaching and learning.

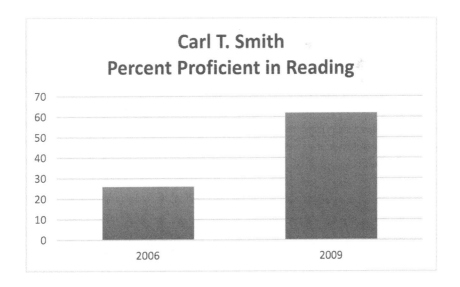

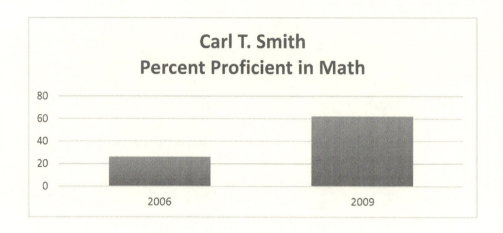

**Carl T. Smith
Percent Proficient in Math**

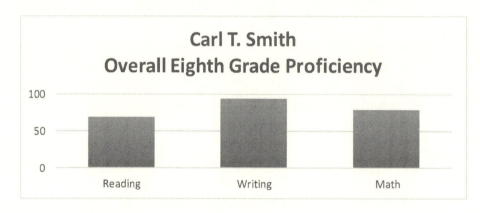

**Carl T. Smith
Overall Eighth Grade Proficiency**

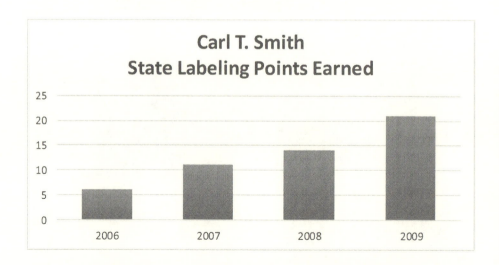

**Carl T. Smith
State Labeling Points Earned**

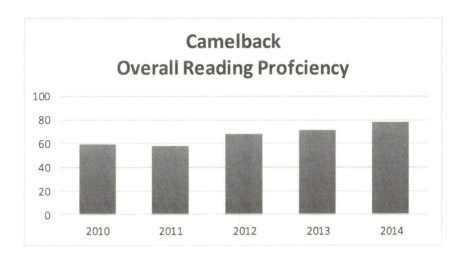

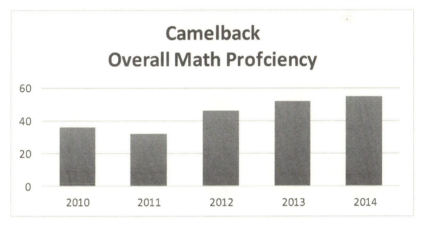

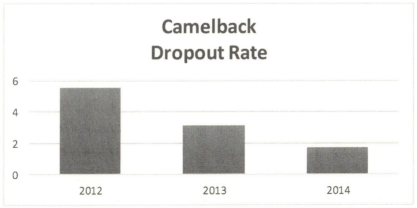

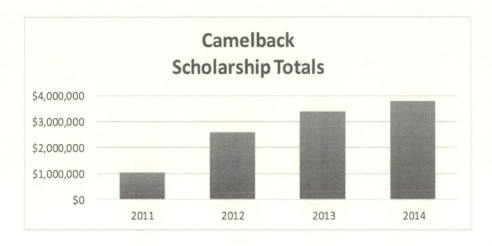

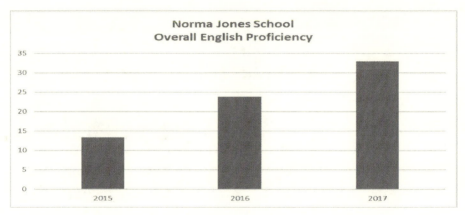

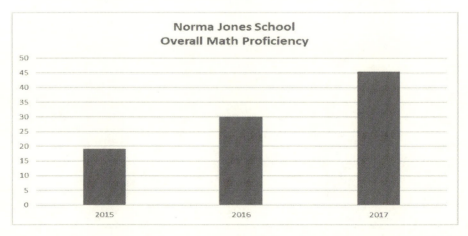

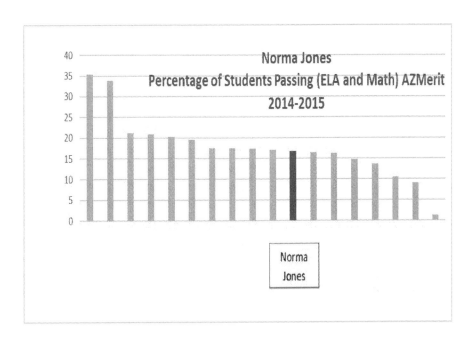

Norma Jones
Percentage of Students Passing (ELA and Math) AZMerit
2014-2015

Norma
Jones

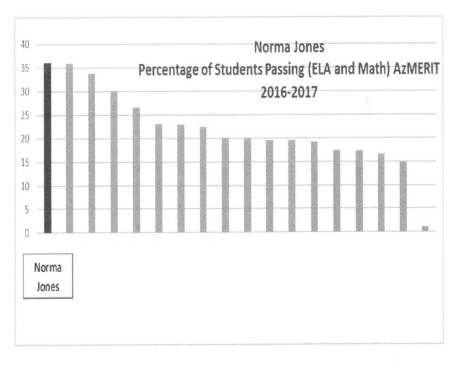

Norma Jones
Percentage of Students Passing (ELA and Math) AzMERIT
2016-2017

Norma
Jones

Over the next few chapters, I use our three principalships, as well as my personal experience as an assistant principal, director, and superintendent, to walk you through the framework using specific examples, suggestions, and real-life stories in an attempt to bring BTL to life and explain how we achieved these results. I will, very transparently, provide you with successes and failures. I will tell you what works and what doesn't. Finally, you will get very practical strategies that you can employ, or teach others to employ, immediately to improve outcomes for students, staff, and community.

One final note – or rather an important leadership lesson – before we immerse ourselves in the model. To this point, and for the remainder of this book, you will see a tremendous amount of "I" and "me" statements versus "we" and "us" statements. Because of the way this book is written – personal examples from my journey, personal experiences from my wife's journey, and advice and insight from mentors and colleagues throughout their respective journeys – it is necessary to distinguish my thoughts and experiences from those of others.

Outside of literature, leading with "I" and "my" is very problematic. Leadership, at its core, is the ability to do work through and with others. It's a team sport, not an individual event. In your staff and community meetings, your emails and newsletters, and your day-to-day interactions with stakeholders, "we," "us," and "our" should be your dominant pronouns, especially when sharing celebrations and progress. Remember Jim Collins' *window versus mirror* leadership perspective. When things are going well, look out a window and give others credit. When things are going badly, look in a mirror, be reflective, and take ownership. In my day-to-day work, presentations, and meeting facilitation, other than when discussing challenges and even failures, you would be hard-pressed to find me using the words "I," "me," and "my" very often. I'd encourage you to do the same.

Chapter 5
Build Relationships
Develop genuine personal and professional relationships with individuals and teams of individuals on campus and in the community

James Kouzes and Barry Posner, in *The Leadership Challenge*, coined the phrase "Leadership is a Relationship." Daniel Goleman in *Primal Leadership* asserts that only 20% of a person's success is based upon IQ and that the other 80% is based on EQ. Emotional Intelligence (EQ) is most commonly assigned a two-part definition. First, it is the ability to recognize, understand and manage our own emotions. Second it is the ability to recognize, understand and influence the emotions of others. In short, EQ is the ability to build and maintain relationships through a greater capacity to communicate, connect with, and inspire others. John Maxwell in *The 21 Irrefutable Laws of Leadership* wrote, "He who thinks he leads, but has no followers, is only taking a walk."

What do these three books, and the leadership lessons they provide, have in common? They make it very clear that relationships, and a leader's ability to maintain them, matter greatly. Without strong relations, leaders are unable to lead and inspire others to action. Without action, there's no progress. Without progress, we don't experience the achievement and performance we all desire for our students. That's why the BTL model starts with relationships. Although there is much more to leadership than making connections with others, I argue in this chapter that there's no better place to start.

Build Relationships Strategy #1: Memorize Faces and Names

After the final interview for the Camelback High School principalship in the spring of 2009, I was called back to the superintendent's office to be formally offered the position. The superintendent and I spent time that afternoon talking about leadership, about the ever-so-important partnership with employee associations, about the loudest and most influential staff and parents in the community, and about the district in general. I used this meeting to glean as much as possible from the superintendent even though he wasn't closely connected to the day-to-day happenings at Camelback. I was able to build some institutional knowledge that I would eventually use in the coming weeks and months. Just as we were wrapping up, he asked if he could do anything else for me.

I answered, "As a matter of fact, I'd love one thing. I'd like to get my hands on the most recent Camelback yearbook you can find – and I'd love it as soon as possible."

The superintendent asked, "Why would you want a yearbook?"

I responded, "To memorize as many faces and names as possible before I meet the staff next month."

When I reflect upon where and when I learned this strategy, I flash back almost 15 years. I was 26. I had just finished three years in the classroom. I probably had no business landing an assistant principalship in a new district, let alone anywhere. I arrived at the elementary school, JB Sutton, completely void of any strategy as to where to begin. As fate or faith would have it, during my first day visiting the campus that summer to meet the principal and office staff, the lead secretary handed me the staff directory. She gave it to me so that I could get a sense of how many staff members we had, who did and taught what, and who I would be responsible for supervising. I still have a clear image of what that directory looked like – just names and categories such as *1st Grade* and *Custodians* and *Crossing Guards*. I eventually could have added my name to the *Crossing Guard* list after I found out my afternoon duty involved crosswalk supervision in front of the school. I remember joking with the secretary about that a few weeks later.

That summer as I prepared to enter into a new community, I decided to memorize all of the names on the directory – 4 males, 79 females (welcome to elementary school). Before my contract started that summer, I knew, by name, job title, and room number, every single person who worked at Sutton. By the time I was introduced to the staff at the first faculty meeting of the year, I was able to very quickly and easily connect names with faces. Interactions would sound something like this:

"Hello, Mr. Gestson. It's nice to meet you. I am Mrs. Johnson."

"Oh it's great to meet you Mrs. Johnson," I'd respond. "I believe you teach 1st grade in room 23, is that correct?"

After just a few days, I knew everyone by face **and** name. I was approached time and time again as the school year launched by various staff to thank me for obviously making an intentional effort to learn everyone's name. To them, it was a sign of respect and dignity. In many ways to me, it was step one in the process of building relationships with so many new people.

I have continued this commitment all throughout my leadership career. When I became the principal at Carl T. Smith, I memorized the staff directory and was able to connect faces and names even quicker because the staff was smaller. When I became the principal at Camelback, I was able to take this effort to the next level. With a school yearbook in hand for the summer, I was able to memorize faces, names, and titles of staff and students. Of course, I'm not superhuman, so I didn't memorize all 225 staff members and 2,000 students in a few weeks, but I was able to show up to campus the first week with teachers and staff and instantly know virtually everyone in some way.

I recall one interaction in particular. It was moments before the first faculty meeting. I happened to bump into a teacher at the bottom of the stairwell on his way up to the library. He stopped me, reached out his hand, and started to introduce himself, "Hey, Dr. Gestson, it's nice to meet you. My name is..."

I quickly yet respectfully cut him off.

"You are Coach Jackson. You teach social studies – AP Economics," I said. "You coach track and cross country. And, two years ago, you were named 'Teacher of the Year" here. I look forward to working with you and learning from you."

He was speechless. He also became one of my biggest supporters for the rest of my tenure at Camelback. And, as you can imagine, I needed as many supporters as possible during the bad days.

This (memorizing names and faces) has become so fundamental to my approach to leadership and relationship-building that when I arrived at the district office four years ago to serve as the Director of School Leadership, I felt it was extremely important to know the names and faces of all 100 or so employees who worked in the district office. What I found out quickly was that the district didn't have a comprehensive directory. So, we created one. In fact, we created a photo directory.

We organized a day when all district office employees came to my office – which for 8 hours was transformed into a private photo studio. We asked cosmetology students from our local high school to come to the district to help employees with their hair and make up. We bought brushes, mini-mirrors, and chocolate. We covered the windows of my office so no one could see inside. Employees could take photos from any angle to make sure they got their "good side." For what it's worth, most wanted the picture taken from above with the photographer standing on a chair. As you may know, it's no longer about the "good side," it's about having no double chin. We told employees that they could take as many pictures as they needed to get the "right one." The result was a great directory that now continues to be updated to this day.

Now if you are one of those people who say, "Oh, I'm just terrible at memorizing people's names," well I have a reaction to that. That's not true. Or, in the least, you can change that if you want. You are not cursed with "bad people memory" – that's not a thing. You likely don't memorize names and faces well because you aren't listening authentically or being intentional. I used to be mediocre at best with faces and names. But then I met an amazing man who not only became a great mentor but also changed the way Megan and I memorize names.

A mentor of mine has the most unbelievable memory of anyone we've ever known. He once ran a 30,000-student school district in Arizona, much like the one I run now, and he knew 100% of the staff in his district by face and name – true story! Unfortunately, I can't claim the same. At that size, that's approximately 3,000 employees. Every time he is asked about his memory, he is quick to say humbly, "Well, you know that memory is the lowest form of intelligence." But when probed, he always gives the same, beautiful response, "I am able to memorize faces and names because I listen with my heart, not my head."

Of course, it's not enough to just memorize faces and names – that's just the start of the relationship-building process. Your knowledge of your staff can't simply be their title and their line of authority. We are in the business of people – and we must know and love them as humans. As Bob Chapman and Raj Sisodia wrote In *Everybody Matters*, every employee is somebody's "precious child." We must treat them as such. In every leadership position that I have held, I have made a commitment to learning all that I can about each individual I work with, lead, supervise, and, ultimately, serve.

Build Relationships Strategy #2: Know and Love Your Staff

At CTS, the staff was much smaller than I was used to –

approximately 40 employees total. Memorizing names and positions took me just a few days. With names in the memory bank, it was time to dig deeper, so I started with a commitment to learning just a few key items about each person. I still remember them to this day: what part of the Valley they lived in, where they grew up, and where they went to high school and/or college. I spent a few weeks, unbeknownst to the staff, gathering this information during random interactions in the hallway, during class visits, during prep periods, and during arrival and dismissal duty. By the end of the first month of school, I knew at least a few key facts about every staff member – and this served as the foundation for future relationship building. My next after-school duty interactions with staff may have then looked something like this:

"So, Mrs. Jackson. You said you are originally from California and went to college there. What brought you to Phoenix?"

"Hey Mr. Gonzalez. Now you told me that you live in the far west valley. Do you have family out there?"

"Since you grew up in Seattle, please tell me that doesn't mean you are a Seahawks fan?" (By the way, we're originally from Seattle and can often be found on Sundays sporting our Hawks gear).

These types of questions allow a leader to learn more about their employees – their lifestyle, their family, their interests, their hopes, and even their struggles.

After Megan was approved by the Board at that contentious meeting, one of her first tasks was to getting to know her staff. She sent out an introductory letter and invited every staff member, from teachers to crossing guards, to sit down and meet with her. She had no agenda for the meetings, just time to put faces to names and get to know each other. Some chose to keep the meetings casual, talking about their work experience and families, while others quickly dove into speaking about strengths and needs of the school.

By the time teachers officially reported back to work, Megan had met with roughly 90% of the staff. This gave her the opportunity to demonstrate the kind of person and leader that she was, and she was able to take the staff's input into consideration when designing the upcoming staff in-service time. Through those one-on-one conversations, she was also able to identify where the strong and weak relationships were among staff and anticipate potential challenges. This would definitely come in handy in the coming months considering her unexpectedly terrible start to the school year.

Although I don't have any formal systems or a specific list of questions to ask, here is a glimpse into the types of information I try to learn about each of my colleagues:

> **Family** – their current family (spouse, kids), their extended family (siblings, parents, grandparents, grandkids), and their pets
>
> **Interests** – travels, hobbies, likes, dislikes, and favorite foods, restaurants, drinks (black coffee or cream and sugar)
>
> **Aspirations** – goals for the future, interest in leadership development, dreams for a higher education, desires and hopes for the school
>
> **Successes and Struggles** – awards won, accomplishments they're proud of, weddings or children in the near future, current struggles such as divorce or bankruptcy, any family tragedies such as loss or illness

All of this information allows a principal to be a better leader for others. If Megan knows that Mr. Johnson has a special needs son, she can be a better leader for him and his family when his son needs extra care at home. If I know that Ms. Jimenez just suffered a painful divorce and is a single mother, I can be a better leader for her and her kids. Ms. Jimenez may even be the first person I ask to help with curriculum writing so that I can assist her financially while she fulfills an important need or duty for the school. Likewise, if Megan knows simple things like Mrs. Rodriguez's parents are coming to town on a Friday afternoon, she can arrange to cover her class 8th period so she can sneak out early to beat the traffic and get the house ready. Again, we are in the people business. We must know and love our staff.

At Camelback, with over 200 employees, this task was much more difficult. It took a lot of time and energy. Luckily, with yearbook in hand, I was able to find a starting place with most employees. I could talk to the band teacher about his passion for music. I could talk to the French teacher about her beautiful accent and her travels abroad. I could ask the AP English Literature teacher about her favorite author. Of course, I didn't have to be armed with any specific information up front to do some relationship-building. Random interactions in the hallway, in the parking lot, and, heck, even in the bathrooms, can provide leaders with enough time to ask questions like, "So, do you have any kids?" or "I see you are wearing a wedding ring, how long have you been married?"

All of these simple day-to-day interactions helped both Megan and me learn as much as possible about the individuals we served. Making mental notes, and even sometimes written or electronic notes, can help a leader memorize important information, especially dates and milestones of significance.

Build Relationships Strategy #3: Remember Milestones

All of us have dates and milestones that are of great significance to us such as birthdays and anniversaries. There are many people who still care deeply about their birthday and want it to be remembered (like our friend, Heather – April 4th). Others are proud of wedding anniversaries (they are often the ones who have flowers delivered to their classrooms once a year on this special date). Still others celebrate milestones like the date they defended their dissertation or were honorably discharged from the military. It doesn't matter which milestone, if particular dates matter to them, they should matter to you.

We must also remember that dates and milestones are not always happy memories for the people we serve. It's the painful milestones that you should be most committed to remembering. The anniversary of the death of a child or a parent, for example, is perhaps the most painful yet important for you to remember. Others remember their sobriety. Others mourn the anniversaries of divorce. Others celebrate remission.

For us, there are dates that matter. Megan was diagnosed with cancer on October 27th many years ago. We never forget that date. She was given a clean bill of health on April 13th. You can bet we don't forget that either. Our anniversary is on July 5th. My brother finally found his sobriety and turned his life over to the Lord on November 17th. Our children were born on August 16th and October 8th. Those matter. Many of you have dates and milestones that matter to you. How amazing would it feel if those around you – especially your "boss" – recognized these dates?

I remember the day that I swung by Ms. Kendrick's classroom during her prep period just to say hi. It happened to be February 29th – leap year. Because it was a unique date, I started our conversation by offering up some uninspiring comment about leap year. Ms. Kendrick suddenly opened up to me that she always dreaded the last day of February.

When I asked her why, she stated, "March is my worst month of the year."

She then went on to tell me that both of her parents died in the month of March just a few years before. The pain was still fresh. The emotion still real. She struggled every year on the eve of March to feel healthy and focused. When March arrived, she dreaded the actual days her parents passed away. She couldn't wait until April. Her March attendance was always terrible. Her referral writing increased. Her spring break lasted more than a week.

You can bet that every March while I was at Camelback, and even when I remember since leaving, that she'd receive an email, a text, or a letter from me on 2/28 or 3/1 letting her know that I was thinking about her. We'd be more patient with her referral writing. We'd prepare to have class coverage before or after spring break.

<u>B</u>uilding Relationships Strategy #4: Weddings Optional, Hospitals Priority, Funerals Non-Negotiable

Megan's experience with cancer was transformative for us for many reasons – one was the realization of how important it is to visit the sick and the mourning. Megan endured chemotherapy, radiation, biopsies, and other intrusive exams for months. The hours in waiting rooms, patient rooms, and in surgery are lonely and stressful. Often, other than a doctor or nurse with a wicked sense of humor, visitors are the only respite. In some ways, it was visitors on those tough days who helped Megan get through that challenging season of her life.

Still today, even with 3,100 employees, I do my best to abide by these rules. If an employee is hospitalized, I will travel to visit or make a phone call. In fact, there have been many times over my career that my first and only interaction with an employee or community member is standing next to a hospital bed or giving a hug. Funerals are even more important. Unless it's not possible, I still attend every funeral I know about. And I am not talking just the deaths of employees – I am talking about employees who have lost spouses, children, siblings, parents. If you can't make the funeral, then you better call or write. And it must be sincere and personal.

It was earlier this year that an employee happened to be parked in front of my district office having a conversation with a colleague. She worked at one of our campuses and was there for a meeting. When she saw me, she immediately got out of her car, walked straight up to me, and gave me a long, emotional hug. You know, the mascara on the jacket type hug. Her son had tragically passed away a few months before. As it turns out, when I heard about her son's death, it was the day of her son's funeral. I called the morning that I heard while she just happened to be on her way to the funeral. She answered the phone suspecting it was a family member. We spoke very briefly that morning.

She was so emotionally numb I wasn't sure she'd even remember. We didn't even talk very long - just enough time for me to say that we had her and her family in our thoughts and prayers, that she had a district family waiting for her when she returned, and that she should take all the time she needed to be healthy before returning. That morning in the parking lot, in each other's embrace, she said that it was one of the most special phone calls she had ever received – and it came at a perfect time.

Megan makes the same commitment. For example, one of her teachers was going through a terrible time at home because of her husband's health. He was in and out of appointments, scans, and exams due to worsening health. Eventually, he was rushed to the hospital where they detected a brain tumor. You can imagine the impact this had on the emotional well-being and work productivity of this employee. One evening, we made time to go visit them in the hospital. We didn't stay long – just long enough for hugs, prayers, and some small talk. Megan and her staff member didn't talk about work or lesson plans. They talked about family, faith, health. In that moment, as Chapman and Sisodia call it, Megan was practicing "truly human leadership."

Perhaps one of the most painful evenings of my professional life was the day that nine of my students were involved in a serious car accident shortly after dismissal on the first Friday of school. Tragically, two students died, two were permanently disabled, and the rest recovered fully. When I heard the news that afternoon, I rushed to the scene of the accident and then to the hospital. I happened to arrive to the hospital before any of the families, so hospital management asked me to help them manage communication with families, and, as traumatic as this sounds, identify the injured students. I spent the entire evening back in the surgery and emergency room areas. I even recall participating in the meeting when the mother of a deceased son found out for the first time. I was the only other person there to help comfort the mother. For the next week, I attended funerals and visited hospitals. I helped lead fundraisers and our staff helped organize funerals. We attended family dinners and memorials. You can only imagine what a pillar of strength my staff and I were for those families during that painful season of their lives.

Build Relationships Strategy #5: Break Bread Together

When Megan was hired as a principal, I remember telling her, "You know, you need to set aside some money now that you are earning a higher salary." Although I don't remember her exact reaction, I'm sure she quickly made some sarcastic comment about more time at Target. But that wasn't the purpose of my advice. What I was talking about was setting aside money for food and drinks for her staff. One of the greatest ways to build relationships and get to know your people is sitting around a table the old fashioned way – eating, drinking, talking.

Granted, I know that you can't afford to take everyone out for lunch or dinner, nor do you have the time. But it is important to make the effort. Over the years, after spending way too much time and money breaking bread together, I have coached new leaders to be much more strategic and intentional in this area, as your time and money is limited. Here is my advice.

Assistant Principals and Coaches: If you have instructional coaches or assistant principals, make time to take them to (or order in) breakfast, lunch, or dinner individually. These are some of the most critical relationships on campus. Don't talk about work – or, if you do, let them take the lead. You want to get to know them – their family, their interests, their goals.

Teacher Leaders and/or Leadership Team: Depending on the teacher leadership structure of your school, you likely have a leadership team of teachers – grade level representatives, department chairs, instructional leaders, etc. During one of your first meetings of the year, organize an early dinner meeting where you all spend time talking and team-building – work can wait until the next meeting.

Employee "Groups": Every campus has various employee "groups" such as office staff, custodial staff, kitchen staff, and a "tech" team if your campus is large enough. All of these people and employee groups matter significantly – as people, as employees, as groups. Ideally, you'd have the time or money to take them all out individually but that's not possible. Arrange for some bread breaking with all of these important groups. Order a pizza dinner with your evening custodial staff – one of the first meals Megan ever had with any of her staff was a taco dinner with her maintenance team that first summer. Buy donuts and bagels for breakfast for your office staff. Have an ice cream party for your tech team. Use this time to sit with teams, ask questions, tell your personal story, and

hear their stories. Everyone on your campus matters –
we must treat them that way.

In my current role, I ultimately oversee 3,100 employees.
It's impossible for me to have breakfast or dinner with all.
Candidly, with my schedule, it's difficult to have a meal with
even a few. So what I recently have started doing is this – I
take every new administrator I hire out for a nice breakfast or
lunch. We get to know each other. We talk about the personal
and professional. We tell stories. And, when the meal is over,
I encourage them to do the same with their people. The hope
is that this spreads and makes its way all throughout the
organization.

I also often encourage school leaders to use summers and
breaks as wisely as possible since finding and making time
throughout the year is so difficult – after all, leaving campus
unsupervised when you don't have to is not a great idea. So,
if you are new principal and got approved at the April or May
board meeting, that means you have 100 days before school
starts and life gets crazy. Use this time to get to know your
people. And, ultimately, if you can't find time for longer
meals, then try liquids.

Build Relationships Strategy #6: From Coffee to Cabernet

Now let me be clear, I have a very strict policy when it
comes to drinking with employees. First of all, if you can't
handle your alcohol, then don't do it in public – especially
with your employees. That's why God made kitchens, family
rooms, and patios. Use those. Second, if you can handle your
alcohol, then adopt a *one and done* strategy. Swing by, say hi,
order a drink, stay long enough to shake a few hands and give
a few hugs, and then leave. Don't be the first one there. Don't
be the last to leave. Be there. Be seen. Be gone. And Uber or
Lyft or taxi home if you have a drink on an empty stomach –

or if you are foolish enough to stay for more than one. $10 Uber or $10,000 DUI, let alone the other official and unofficial consequences?

Now that we've established the rules, I have to be honest for a moment. Remember in a previous chapter when I explained that I would share both successes and failures as a leader? Here is one of those moments.

I did not always have drinking rules. In fact, I think I broke every drinking rule imaginable while serving as the principal at CTS. Now, don't worry, nothing bad ever happened. And, to be fair, if you knew me, you'd know that I'm terribly boring and live a very simple, calculated life. So when I say I broke every rule, I don't actually mean *every* rule. But what I do mean is this. While I was the principal at CTS, I not only attended *happy hours*, I hosted them. I wouldn't stay for one. I'd do two. I'd be the last to leave. We even once hosted a staff Christmas party where my staff and I played beer pong, as a staff, on a piece of plywood that had "CTS" *sharpied* in the middle. And when I say "as a staff," I don't mean a small clique. I mean the entire staff.

The turning point for me was the next morning after a big gathering at our house – it probably wasn't the beer pong night. And, yes, that means we hosted more than one large party. Our daughter was old enough to speak by this time. That morning, as we were in the back room of our house drinking morning coffee (and, mind you, we don't have a large house), our daughter walks in the room and says, "Dad, is that one of your teachers asleep on your couch?"

Sure enough, I walk into the other room, and there on one of our couches is an employee. Now, to be fair, our staff did have a no drinking and driving rule. And this teacher had adhered to that rule. But it was at that point that I created a new rule – no house parties. Since that time, I've created many other drinking rules. And, since that time, I always stick to them.

When I say *From Coffee to Cabernet*, I actually don't exclusively mean *happy hours*. I actually avoid large group *happy hours* now. What I'm talking about is quick one-on-ones with key people. You may not have time to take someone to breakfast but you can drive them through the Starbucks line. You may not have time to do dinner but you may have time to grab a local craft beer or a glass of wine on your way home. Did I say Uber?

At Norma Jones, many of Megan's teachers take on a significant amount of leadership, especially in planning and leading school events, since they are now without an assistant principal due to budget cuts. Several of her teacher leaders are aspiring administrators as well. Budgetary restraints limit how Megan is able to compensate them for their extra time and energy, so she has found opportunities to express her gratitude and provide one-on-one time for talking leadership through occasional happy hours.

Camelback High School is located near many local coffee shops – a drive-through Starbucks, a locally-owned cafe, and a few other breakfast and bakery joints. From time to time, I would block off a half hour on my schedule to take someone to grab a quick coffee. Sometimes we'd sit for 15 minutes and just talk. Sometimes we'd drive the neighborhood to remind ourselves where our students lived. Sometimes we'd head back to the office and just sit for 10 minutes. Thirty minutes, $6, and priceless relationship-building.

Likewise, *happy hour*, if you can abide by "the rules," is an easy way to spend 30 minutes with someone on your radar – a new employee, a local business owner, an employee who has seemed down as of late, a teacher that needs to feel special.

Still today, in my current role, I will often have my assistant schedule quick *happy hour* meetings with one to two people. There are many times I won't even have an alcoholic beverage. Just the act of getting off site, being in a relaxed setting, and connecting through stories and values is such a great way to build relationships or even do business.

Chapter 6
Enhance Your Institutional Knowledge
Understand the history, relationships, power structures, systems, points of pride, areas of frustration, and dreams and aspirations of a wide variety of stakeholders

If only school leadership was just about pizza, Starbucks, and beer pong. Unfortunately, it's much more complex and requires much more intentionality. Relationships are truly foundational. That's why we start there. I believe that you can't and won't create sustainable, authentic change if you haven't first reached your people on a personal level.

In an effort to manage their time efficiently, effective leaders can also use relationship-building with stakeholders as a means to gain valuable insight into what works, what doesn't, what needs to be fixed, and what needs to change. In most governmental agencies, this is called "intelligence." Intelligence helps leaders understand what decisions should be made and which ones should be avoided. Intelligence helps leaders know what motivates their staff. Intelligence can also help a school leader shift culture and climate and, eventually, student achievement.

Enhance Your Institutional Knowledge Strategy #7: Become the Chief Historian

"What are you going to do to get the Madison kids back?" seemed like a simple enough question. After all, they surely wouldn't ask a racially-charged question during a public principal forum, would they? Well, they did, and luckily for me, my answer was generic and innocent enough not to have gotten any real reaction.

In the "meeting after the meeting" (by the way, usually the most important part of any meeting are the meetings that take place in the hallways and in the parking lots at the conclusion), a teacher approached me on my way to my car.

"Dr. Gestson. Excuse me. I just have to ask. Do you know what they meant when they asked about the Madison kids?" she asked.

Naively I remarked, "Well, sure, Camelback's enrollment is down nearly a 1,000 students since the 90's and they want enrollment back up to where it used to be."

"Although that's true, that's not what they were asking," she said. "You see, Camelback used to be an all-white, upper-middle class school through the 1990's. Since that time, because of a desegregation court order, the school's demographics have shifted completely. As you know, Camelback is now a Title I school serving almost exclusively Latino and African-American students. Many of these teachers who are still here were hired in the 1990's to teach in a predominantly white school. They don't like the diversity. They don't embrace the challenges and opportunities of teaching urban youth. When they asked you how you were going to get Madison students back, they were asking how you planned to bring back white wealthy kids from the north in hopes of getting rid of poor Latino and African-American students from the south."

"Well that would have been nice to know an hour ago," I responded, with both humor and embarrassment.

"Oh don't worry. You answered the question just fine in there. I just wanted to let you know what you are getting yourself into," she said as she turned away and walked toward her car.

For the next few months, I went on a mission. My mission was simple – to become the *Chief Historian* of Camelback High School. My goal was to know more about the past, present, and future of the school than anyone else on that campus. I wanted to know the good, the bad, and the ugly. At the time, I felt it was necessary to my survival.

My perspective on becoming the chief historian has evolved over the years. I often teach that the goal of a new leader is to do so much reading and research on the past and present of the school that a leader feels complete ownership of the school even before the first faculty meeting. The leader must feel as though she or he is a part of the community, not a visitor or the new neighbor next door. Simply put, between the time a leader is hired and the time a leader delivers the opening message at the first staff meeting, the leader should be able to speak comfortably in the "we" and "our" form, not the "you" and "your."

Here's the difference.

"We" and "Our"

"Good morning everyone. I am so excited to be here today and am so honored and humbled to join this family and serve our community with you. I believe very strongly that we have such potential here because of our amazing people and programs. Granted, we have a long way to go. But, collectively, we have the right people and programs to create amazing change for our kids."

"You" and "Your"

"Good morning everyone. Thanks for coming. I am proud to be your new principal. You all have a great school here. You have great people and programs. You know as well as I do that we have some tough work ahead of us. But, based on my interactions with a few of you, you have the commitment necessary to do great work for your kids."

Either of those sound familiar? Whether or not they do, one thing is certain. Most staff members would leave awfully uninspired if a new leader showed up to the first meeting having what seemed to be no personal connection with the school. Conversely, how amazing would it be as a teacher or office staff member if they felt as though the new principal was completely and personally invested in the school by day one?

Of course, there is no science to becoming the chief historian, it simply takes work, time, focus. Below, I have outlined some important questions to research. Of course, there are many other questions to be asked and answered. This just gives you a start.

General History
When was the school founded?
Does it have a unique history (changing demographics, school closures, major recognitions or tragedies, etc?)
Did it have any "glory years" or "dark years?"
Are there any prominent alumni?

Leadership History
How many principals have there been in recent history?
Have previous leaders been loved or hated? Why?
Are current leaders (assistant principals, department chairs, districts office leaders) loved or hated? Why?
Are there are major decisions that leadership has made recently that have been applauded or hated?

Academic History
What is the performance history of the school? Is the current performance a recent phenomenon or is it consistent?
Are there programs, initiatives, or curriculum that the staff loves or hates?

Athletics, Arts, Activities History
Is or was the school known for any sports or arts?
Have there been any state championships in sports, clubs (such as chess), or arts?

Has the school produced any professional athletes or artists?
Are there programs that we were once great and now are floundering (or no longer around)?

Building History
Are the buildings old or new?
Have there been buildings, classrooms, or bathrooms that have been neglected?
Are there "bad" classrooms and "good" classrooms (teachers often have strong opinions about this)?

Behavioral History
How do the students behave? Is the current behavior consistent with past behavior?
Are there discipline programs or initiatives in place that are working or not working?
What programs or initiatives have been tried and did they succeed or fail?
What are the typical types of behaviors seen or experienced on the campus?

These, and other questions, are critically important to know before a leader begins to fix problems or create change. Often, a leader can build off recent momentum or, contrariwise, avoid the pitfalls of the past failures. Which leads us to our next Strategy.

<u>E</u>nhance Your Institutional Knowledge Strategy #8: At All Your "Firsts," Listen More Than You Speak

I recently sat through a leadership team meeting at one of my campuses. There were seven people around the table – a new principal, four veteran assistant principals, an instructional coach, and me. The new principal is naturally an amazing leader and is going to thrive for many years to come

– of that I'm confident. But in this first meeting, I was reminded why listening is so important.

This particular day happened to be the first "PLC" Wednesday of the year. All district office leaders – including the superintendent – are required to visit campuses, observe PLCs in action, and then sit through the "Admin Debrief" meeting when PLCs end for the day. This particular team sat around the table talking about observations that morning. They weren't happy with what they saw in a few PLCs. Some teams got started 15 minutes late. Others operated more like department meetings rather than PLCs. The principal began to talk about some changes that she'd like to see in the coming weeks. She made suggestions about some books that the school needed to read and strategies they needed to adopt. She talked about some structure changes that were going to have to change by the end of the month. She even started to suggest some timelines.

I could feel the energy in the room change. The rest of the leadership team got quiet. They started to look around the table at each other. No one made eye contact with the new principal. One assistant principal even started checking email on his phone. So, I inserted myself.

"I'm just going to be honest. The room just got very quiet. I am going to guess that some of the strategies that Mrs. Valdez just suggested have been tried before – or are currently in place but just looked sloppy today. Am I right?" I asked.

One brave soul, an assistant principal, not wanting to appear to be disrespectful to the new, talented principal, said, "Well, actually, that's right …"

The team went on to give the principal one big history lesson on the past, present, and future plans of PLC's at the school. Many of the items that she had suggested had already been tried and failed. Some had been implemented, were showing progress, but just weren't in place on this particular day. One of the two books she suggested had already been read by PLC leaders. After a productive conversation, and some new knowledge and perspective, the team created some simple next steps for PLCs and then moved on to other issues like lunch duty and the staff meeting later that week.

As a leader, you are going to attend many "firsts" – first faculty meeting, first parent meeting, first admin meeting (if you have an admin team), first parent-teacher conference, first home football game. For some reason, so many leaders believe that their "firsts" must consist of them establishing expectations, making sure people know how smart they are, showing the staff who is boss, and so forth. That is not true at all. A leader's firsts must be primarily listening sessions, not lecturing sessions. As a leader you want to learn about the history of faculty meetings before you re-structure them or take them over. You want to know how home football games are run before changing the concession stand location. You want to observe an evening of parent-teacher conferences before proposing a new model.

Listening during firsts helps a leader avoid trouble, earns the respect of those in attendance, and ripens the soil for changes later. At Megan's first introductory meeting with available staff members during the summer, she brought a simple T-chart with 2 questions for the group: What's working? What's not? The two simple questions allowed staff members to speak freely about their perceptions of the school. As hard as it was to not jump into discussing solutions to problems, Megan limited her speaking time and took copious notes. She asked probing questions when appropriate, but also did so in a way that didn't cast judgment or cause friction among staff members. She wanted people to feel comfortable in sharing their thoughts and opinions. Later that year when she introduced her first set of initiatives, she was able to refer directly to the input of the staff for rationale behind the decision. (Most of these initiatives were *fixables*, which you will learn more about in the next chapter.)

Megan also quickly learned that several staff members had been at the school for nearly 30 years. Their willingness to share their knowledge and experiences allowed Megan to gain a strong understanding of the school's history. These valuable educators had taught generations of families and were greatly respected in the community. If she hoped to gain the respect and trust of the school's students and families, time spent listening to her new colleagues' stories (even 2-3 times) was time well-spent.

Enhance Your Institutional Knowledge Strategy #9: Host Community Stakeholder Meetings (or Join Theirs)

The perspective of a faculty and staff is arguably the most important and most useful for a new leader. They live the work every day – many up to 10-12 hours a day. They know the kids, the climate, the culture, the systems, the successes, the skeletons in the closet. They are the change-makers and the anchors.

Often, however, staff can also lack the perspective of the outside world. They get mired down in their work. Teachers close their doors and teach 6-7 hours a day and, as a teacher recently told me, "I just don't get out much. I have too much work to do to socialize on campus." Because of this, their world and their perspective, can easily become narrowed.

In order to get a really clear picture of the school – its reputation, its support, its stature in the community – it is vital that a leader expand listening sessions to the outside community. The easiest way to do this is to host community forums and stakeholder meetings. The purpose of these forums and meetings is three-fold:

First, these are relationship-building exercises. Taking time to get to know your community – the major players, the loudest parents, and the most supportive neighbors – is essential. This intelligence will all come in handy later.

Second, you have to remember that your community needs to know and respect you, too. These investments in relationship-building aren't just about you and what you need to know and be able to do. New leaders need to build some "street cred," if you will. The only way to do this is to hit the streets, or bring the streets to you.

Third, these meetings are another vital step in learning about the history and context of the school. Often, you'll learn information that you need for a meeting the next week; often you'll even learn information you didn't think you needed to know.

When I first arrived to Camelback, it drove me absolutely crazy that the school had been painted in two different phases over two different decades. Half of the school was a beautiful new blend of orange, blue, and red. The other half of the school was old, stale, faded white. As I asked around campus, nobody had a good answer for why the district only painted half of the school. This had become so bothersome to me that I had scheduled a meeting with the district facilities director to put a plan in place to get the rest of the school painted. In some ways, I was ready to be forceful about it. To me, it was that ugly. Parents, especially high school parents, care deeply about the look and feel of a campus. If Camelback's enrollment was down hundreds of students over the past decade, a facelift may help build some hype and momentum in the community. I was certain a new paint job would be seen as a huge victory throughout the community.

At the community forum the week before this big meeting with the facilities department, after asking a series of questions of the community, I proudly made an announcement that I was putting together plans to complete the exterior painting of the school. In an instant, there was a split reaction within the crowd. Half of the group applauded. The other half became very angry and vocal. As it turns out – and yet another reason why community stakeholder meetings are critical – it was the community that put a stop to the second half of the paint job. A few years before, when the district began painting the campus, the neighbors began to create a raucous because they felt the new colors made the school look like a "Harkins Theater," not a school. Neighbors complained that that it would decrease property values and would attract graffiti. Others who knew more about painting in the desert claimed (and were right) that bright, vibrant colors in sunny Phoenix would fade quickly. After enough community pressure, the district decided to stop the painting project. Just a few years later, I was just about to step into a hornet's nest, and I would not have known had I not intentionally scheduled these meetings.

Parents and guardians aren't the only external stakeholders that matter. As you coordinate various meetings, be sure to take into account the following groups of people:

> **Neighbors and Community Members:** Neighbors within walking distance of your school, even those who don't have children who attend your school, often have a lot to say about your school, your students, your arrival, your dismissals, and especially your sporting and band events (for middle schools and high schools).

> **Block Watches, HOAs, and Other Neighborhood Groups:** Sometimes it is easier to attend existing meetings in the community instead of you hosting your own. When I first started at Camelback, I attended every Block Watch and HOA meeting I could find just to introduce myself and humanize the school as best as possible. This investment of time was useful later when my students tagged alleys and neighbors' property.

> **Alumni Groups:** This may be less relevant in K-8, but often high schools have very active alumni groups.

These are easy places to plug into and also a great opportunity to engage people who already have a personal, vested interest in the school.

Feeder and Partner Schools and Districts: Depending on the grades of your school, this may be more or less helpful. If you lead a middle school, you should build relations with and know as much about your feeder elementary school or your partner high school, for example.

Business Leaders: Many local businesses not only can offer feedback, they can also offer resources. Tap into these early. If you don't know who your local business and community leaders are, take a drive.

Enhance Your Institutional Knowledge Strategy #10: Drive the Neighborhood

One of the simplest yet most impactful activities a new leader can do is drive the neighborhood – early and often. In fact, this is not only an activity for the leader, it can be a powerful activity for the entire staff.

It was one of my first early release faculty meetings at Camelback. Because of the history at Camelback (desegregation, ever-changing demographics, extreme variation in wealth, to name a few), I decided to cancel a September faculty meeting and instead have every teacher on campus do home visits. I asked 125 teachers to drive into the poorest and most dangerous parts of the school community and visit the homes, trailers, apartments, and projects of the students. As you can imagine, this was met with mixed emotions – from "This will be amazing!" to "I'll go if I can drive with a strong male teacher." to "Hell, no. I won't go even if you discipline me!"

Despite the mixed reactions, I moved forward with the plan. For those "Hell, no" teachers, I decided that the admin team would drive with them (turns out it was really about fear, not about resistance). I encouraged the staff to pick 1-2 students each and, unlike a typical "bad news" home visits, I encouraged them to do "good news" home visits. What a treat it would be to have a high school teacher knock on your door to tell you that your teenage son is a pleasure to have in class.

Of course, the ultimate goal of the home visits wasn't even about the messages delivered to parents that day (although that was a very powerful experience). The goal was to gain perspective and empathy. It was to get a better understanding of the living conditions of even our best performing students. It was to remind teachers that, although the school was geographically located in a nice middle-class neighborhood, our students lived in much different conditions.

While I was at CTS, I took time every single morning to drive at least one portion of our neighborhood. This would often only take me 5 extra minutes. I did this for three reasons. First, I wanted to make sure nothing tragic had happened in the neighborhood overnight like a house fire or a murder. Second, I always tried to pull over to say hi to one community member – a student who was up early, a parent working in the yard, a community member walking the dog. I wanted the community to see *the principal* actively engaged in and committed to the broader community. Finally, I was looking for new graffiti. For one, I wanted to know if there were any new gangs or gang activity in the area. For two, the City of Phoenix had a graffiti removal hotline that any citizen could call to report graffiti. I wanted to make sure that the area surrounding the school remained graffiti-free.

There are other reasons why leaders and staff should drive the neighborhood – not just for home visits. There are businesses that may want to donate money. There are parks that could be good for field trips (or fights). There are churches that provide support services. There are libraries that stay open on weekends. There are restaurants that would be willing to donate food. Schools are a vital part of a community, and it's extremely important that school leaders know what people, places, and resources exist in the community that their school serves. If anything, driving the neighborhood is a great way for the community to see and meet the principal. So grab a stack of business cards and hit the road. You'll find that there is virtually no-one in the community who doesn't like to meet and interact with the local school principal. And the more you meet, the larger your network of supporters.

$\underline{E}$nhance Your Institutional Knowledge Strategy #11: Attend Everything

Okay. Not quite everything. But as much of and as many as is possible.

Before I go into much detail, it is important to note that life balance is critically important. When I teach classes or present publicly about leadership, I almost always end with a lesson on life balance, which typically includes a lecture about 6 F's (faith, family, fitness, finances, fun, future) and 2 B's (balance, boundaries). In some ways, this strategy is a bit hypocritical. However, in a leader's first year, there just truly isn't much balance if you want to do it right. Balance is a goal for the 2nd or 3rd year.

The primary reason it's critical to *Attend Everything* is because you need to see and experience everything firsthand before you can make intelligent decisions about anything. How can you make a major change to a parking lot traffic issue if you don't do arrival and dismissal duty for a week?

Attending everything your first year is also critically important from a visibility perspective. Staff, students, parents, and community want to see the principal everywhere. Politically speaking, parents and community don't care if your assistant principal covers an event – to them, that doesn't count. They want to see the principal. They want to interact with the principal. They want to get to know, like, and respect the principal. They also want to be known by the principal. Candidly, attending everything is not a realistic or even fair expectation, but for the first year, it's definitely worth the investment of time.

Although this may be obvious, below is a list of events you should attend your first year. Keep in mind, the objective of attending events, aside from making personal connections with attendees, is to gather intelligence and gain firsthand knowledge to make informed decisions later when you need to fix problems or create change.

> **Sporting Events:** For middle school and high school, it's not enough to attend Friday night football games or rivalry basketball games. You must attend cross country meets, golf tournaments, and tennis matches.

> **Arts Performances:** For leaders, K-12, these range from the cute 2nd grade holiday performance to the high school dance recital.

> **Recess:** Even if "recess duty" isn't officially on your calendar, it is important to spend time observing behaviors of students and staff, watching patterns and trends, and making note of the types of activities and equipment student use. This information will help later when dealing with playground issues.

> **Lunch:** First of all, even if you don't think that lunch duty should be the task of a principal, I'd argue that you should make this a daily duty your first year at least. Of course, there will be days when you have to miss, but it is critically important that principals have a

strong pulse on lunch time behaviors – eating habits (do they waste a lot of food or always skip the pizza), manners and cleanliness (do kids throw away food or treat the lunch assistants with respect), and transitions (do kids sprint to the playground or walk in an orderly fashion). Also, as you probably know by now, lunch-time referrals take up the vast majority of an administrator's time handling discipline, so observing lunch behavior issues firsthand is also important. Reductions to lunch referrals equates to increases in classroom time.

Arrival and Dismissal: Finally, it is very important that you have a strong handle on arrival and dismissal time. More often than not, especially in elementary schools and middle schools (yet often in high schools as well), arrival and dismissal issues will be one of the first issues you will need to tackle as a principal.

Enhance Your Institutional Knowledge Strategy #12: Go See the Nurse

As a school leader, it is very easy to forget how important your classified and other support staff are to the success and operations of the school. Loud parents, student discipline, teaching and learning issues, and teacher evaluations can easily consume your mind and control your calendar. However, students, parents, and teachers aren't the only important people on your campus. Your crossing guards keep your students safe in the morning. Your cafeteria staff serves 1-2 meals every day to every student. Your counselors create schedules and help students with college and scholarship applications. As such, it is important to know and experience their work as well.

When I first became an assistant principal, I was assigned every classified staff member to supervise and evaluate – a typical assistant principal assignment. To make sure that I knew my people and understood their work, I made a commitment to spend time with each major employee group. I spent an entire lunch period in the cafeteria. I stood in the front office during arrival and dismissal to see how the office staff managed the community. I even remember going back to work around 9PM one night to spend a couple hours with the night custodial crew. Not only did I develop a clearer understanding of their roles and responsibilities, I was able to build relationships and earn the respect of staff that had likely been largely ignored in the past.

I also remember the day that my nurse at Camelback High School brought forth a concern about an overcrowded office during Advisory and lunch. Yes, Camelback was lucky enough to have a nurse yet only had one for over 2,000 students and 200 employees. Instead of making a quick decision about rules in the nurse's office during Advisory and lunch, I took time to go visit the nurse's office. I wanted to see how busy it was, what types of issues students had, if there was a need for more seating or supplies, and so on. What I learned that day was that the nurse was so busy (and so dedicated) that she never took a lunch. The students' lunch period was her lunch period, and Camelback had never created a schedule for the Health Center that allowed the nurse to eat her own lunch. So, after observing and getting feedback, I made a decision to close her office every day for 7th period. Of course, if an emergency occurred, she would see students. But, more often than not, she had an interruption-free lunch time, and I had another champion in my corner.

Here are a few individuals, groups, or areas that a principal should consider observing: the nurse, custodians (day and night), kitchen staff (breakfast and lunch), office staff, assistant principal's office or area, the counseling center, and other areas of campus such as a performing arts center, the physical trainer's office, the weight rooms, the gymnasiums, and the library.

Enhance Your Institutional Knowledge Strategy #13: Map the Power, Political, and Personal Structures of the School

One of the most powerful activities that a new leader can do is map out the power, political, and personal structures of the school. Of course, this can only happen after weeks and months of listening and observing. But it is critically important to a leader's success to know who is related to who, who listens to who, who likes (and doesn't) like who, who is dating (or dated) who, and who has earned or lost the respect of who.

I often tell a story about a teacher, Mr. Thomason, who had more power than I did for the first three years of my tenure at Camelback. If Mr. Thomason didn't like, respect, or buy in to one of my ideas, he could get enough support from others to shut down the idea. Likewise, if he loved and supported an idea, he would make sure it was successful. It took me about a year to figure this out. And when I did, it caused me to ask a question, "I wonder if there are other people on this campus who are more powerful than me?" So, for the first time in my life, I began to map out the power structures of the school.

Much like an organizational chart, I began with the name of an influential employee. Below that employee, I created categories of people, departments, and/or teams that were influenced by that employee. Then, when applicable, I also noted categories of people who were influenced by those people, departments, or teams. I would often even go one layer below that (see below). What I found was that one person could easily have influence and power over 50 to even 100 people on a campus.

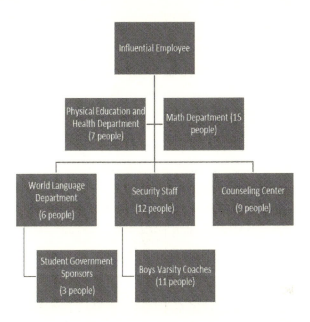

After mapping out the power and political structure of the school, I came to the conclusion that there were about 5 people on the campus (out of 225) that had influence, and even control, over 200 people. On one hand, that was a very scary realization. On the other hand, it made the decision-making and implementation process much easier. If I could get those 5 on board, I could get all 200. If I couldn't get those 5 on board, then the idea or initiative was a "no go."

I also found great benefit to mapping out personal structures as well. I mapped out who on campus was related. I mapped out who was dating or married (or had dated or had been married). I made a list of friends and foes. I even made note of which employees lived in the neighborhood or were related to key members of the community. Knowing these personal connections or structures helped me when it came time to make decisions or even triangulate communication about key initiatives or changes. As an example, I once changed the drop-off and pick-up location of special education buses. I knew that the neighbors to the north wouldn't be happy. But I also knew that the loudest neighbor was cousins with one of my night custodians. So, I had that custodian deliver the message (the what, the why, the when). I never even had to make a formal announcement or schedule a community meeting.

As I mentioned earlier, Megan had several staff members who had been at the school for an exceptionally long time. In addition to that, she also had a few staff members who were students themselves in the school, or currently had children enrolled in the school and lived in the community. Whenever she made a change that would impact families, such as revising the student drop-off/pick-up routine, adding fencing, or installing a new digital visitor management system, she made sure to connect with the staff members closest to the community. She sought their opinions and questions and then ensured that they had all the information needed in order to message the changes in the most positive way.

These last two chapters – *Build Relationships* and *Enhance Your Institutional Knowledge* – are foundational in so many ways. Relationships and knowledge ("intelligence") allow a leader to motivate others, avoid and solve problems, build momentum, gain credibility, and so much more. The thirteen specific Strategies you just read about were designed to help leaders discern what is broken and what isn't, what works and what doesn't, and what needs to be fixed and what needs to be changed (those are very different and we'll explain why in the next chapter). This intelligence serves as the launching pad for the next chapter.

Chapter 7
Fix the Fixables (Don't Create Change)
Find solutions to simple, surface-level problems that improve working and learning conditions as well as build the momentum and credibility necessary for real change (later)

In 2012, the Harvard Business Review published an article titled, *Ten Reasons People Resist Change*. Among the top ten were a few that are very relevant to this chapter and education in general. One was the fear (and often reality) that change means more work. Often, even if the change yields better results, it often means more work. Another was concerns about competence – employees often wonder if they (personally) are competent enough to navigate the change while others wonder if their leadership is able to lead the change. A third reason employees resist change is that past "changes" were painful or not effective. People question if this will be yet another failed attempt at change. The author even suggests a remedy: "Leaders should consider gestures to heal the past before sailing into the future."

Although the idea of *Fix the Fixables* wasn't designed to be a remedy to heal all past harm, it is designed to fulfill a similar purpose. Leaders today have to remember that educators, especially teachers, are very stressed and, in most cases, overworked and underappreciated. They spend 6-7 straight hours with few, if any breaks. Many don't have time to use the restroom, let alone enjoy a relaxing uninterrupted lunch. We require them to do arrival and dismissal duty, give up prep periods to look at data, engage in parent meetings after school, and make phone calls in between classes. The fact of the matter is, principals and teachers have much different worries and wants:

Principals are worried about the quality of PLCs.
Teachers want their prep period back.

Principals want more effective instructional practices. Teachers don't want to complete lesson plans.

Principals want teachers up and active every minute of the day. Teachers don't want to take time during the day to beg for more dry erase markers and paper.

Principals want paperwork turned in on time. Teachers want access to the copy machines. They also don't want to have to punch in a copy code so that admin can monitor their copy machine behaviors. That's offensive to professionals.

Principals want every teacher to arrive to work on time, fully prepared, ready to teach. Teachers just want a good parking spot.

I often wonder why it is that principals and school leaders – year after year, decade after decade – think that their wants and worries are more important than that of their teachers and staff. I have argued this point with many principals over the years (who think that teachers should essentially give up all happiness to improve student achievement). I remember a conversation I once had with a principal who was very stuck in his ways. I said,

"With all due respect, let me remind you of a few important facts. You don't register students in the front office. You don't cook food in the cafeteria. You don't cross students at the crosswalks (well, sometimes). You don't coach sports teams. You don't direct the school play. You don't run interventions. You don't vacuum classrooms. You don't teach economics. You don't "do" anything. You lead everything. You get paid to talk and make decisions. So, from now on, keeping in mind you talk for a living and everyone else on your campus does the real work, I suggest you worry about their needs just as much as those of your students. The bottom line is, if you meet their needs, they'll meet your students' needs."

It is important to note that worrying about teachers' needs has nothing to do with a principal trying to be liked by her or his staff. Although one can argue that "likeability" goes a long way, leadership is not about people pleasing. In fact, as many leaders have said over time (in one variation or another), "the quickest way to failure is to try to please everyone." Instead, worrying about teachers' needs is four-fold.

Happy Employees Are Hard-Working Employees: Decades of research and studies of successful businesses show that companies that focus on working climate and conditions have stronger performance and outcomes. Don't agree? Read *Happiness Advantage*.

Remove Distractions and Barriers to Success: Often, leaders unknowingly create (or ignore) barriers to success and productivity. Remove barriers, improve performance. Want a great read about removing barriers? Try the book *Switch*.

Credibility and Momentum: People follow leaders that they like, trust, and respect. They also follow leaders who are competent, have a plan, and have proven their worth and ability. If you haven't read *Leading Change*, you'll see what I mean.

You Scratch My Back, I'll Scratch Yours: This is self-explanatory. No books needed for this. If I'm nice to you, typically you are nice to me. I do a favor for you, typically you'll do a favor for me. As Franklin Delano

Roosevelt once said, "If you treat people right, they'll treat you right .. about 90% of the time."

Ultimately, in this particular phase of school leadership, the goal is to fix problems and avoid making change. As we'll mention briefly later, people hate change. They love to have problems fixed and barriers removed, but they hate more change – especially veteran teachers. Veteran teachers and staff have usually experienced and worked for many leaders. Each new leader brings new ideas and initiatives. Of course, the principal is excited about these potential improvements, but the veteran staff has a much different perspective – yet another leader with new ideas to solve education that ultimately won't make a real impact. That's why fixing the fixables is phase one. Creating change is phase two.

Every school leader, especially those who have been intentional about listening, could make a list of a hundred problems that need to be solved. Some of those problems are simple and can be solved in ten minutes or with ten dollars (like a clock). Others are slightly more complicated but only require a little team work and a little planning to solve (like a new playground duty schedule). Others are very complicated and will take serious time and commitment. All of these are important, but for the sake of this chapter, we will focus on the first two – the simple and the slightly more complicated. The serious problems – the design of the cafeteria, the irrigation problems on the football field, or the need for a new crosswalk in the community – can and should wait until later.

Fix the Fixables Strategy #14: Find the Short-Term Wins

In the first chapter, I described the mess that I walked into when I took over Carl T. Smith Middle School. Gangs, drugs, violence, disrespect, and academic apathy, to name a few, plagued the school. The staff were miserable and the administration just couldn't gain any momentum. After it was announced that the current principal was leaving and I was coming, the staff got together to draft a document titled, "12 Things the New Principal Should Consider." As mentioned before, it was a well-thought out document. In fact, my staff and I eventually implemented many of their suggestions. The first time I read the list, I was shocked (and happy) to find the 12th item on the list was, "Clock for the Staff Workroom." I knew right away what my first victory would be. I had just finished reading Rudy Giuliani's book, *Leadership*, that talked about the importance of short-term victories and early wins.

In preparation for my first staff meeting, I drove to Target to buy a nice, large clock for the workroom. I bought a battery and set the time. I then grabbed a hammer and a nail and made sure I arrived early to the staff meeting. I snuck back to the workroom, picked the perfect location for the clock, hammered in the nail, and then hid the clock in the cabinet below.

Over the next 15-20 minutes, staff members made their way into the workroom. Many came up to introduce themselves. Others sat in the back and opted not to say hello – you know, those skeptics who don't trust anybody. I made sure I talked to them after the meeting.

I then began the meeting by introducing myself, thanking them for their time and their commitment, and expressing gratitude for making time to create such a detailed list of 12 recommendations. I then spent the next 20-30 minutes going recommendation by recommendation, sharing thoughts and reactions to each. I made my way down the list, from 1-11. When I finished the 11th item, I purposefully stopped short of the 12th – the clock. I then began to wrap up the meeting, thanking them for their input and questions that afternoon. I instantly began to hear grumbling in the back of the room. People became upset and even angry that I had ignored the clock recommendation. The grumbling got louder and louder until a staff member finally raised her hand. "Excuse me. Many of us can't help but notice that you ignored our last recommendation. That one was really important to us. We can't believe you'd overlook it. We've been asking for a clock in here for two years. This is really disappointing to us."

"Oh, that's right," I commented after the tension in the room was plenty thick. "I'm sorry about that. I actually have your clock right here." I then opened the cabinet, took out the new clock (already set to the right time), climbed on the counter, and hung the clock on the pre-hung nail." I had my first victory.

Norma Jones was one of the oldest schools in the district, constructed in the 1960s, and hadn't seen many renovations in the half-century since it was built. All of the original window bays on the classrooms had either been covered up with stucco, or the windows had been painted over. A few years prior to Megan's arrival, the campus was the "beneficiary" of a community service project that involved a significant amount of paint. All of those window bays were repainted in either bright yellow, lime green, or royal blue. Despite the good intentions of the volunteers, the buildings looked worse after the project than they did before.

Megan immediately reached out to her superintendent and district facilities department for assistance. In the recent years, virtually all of the other schools in the district had received some type of painting upgrade, even though Jones had been passed by. Megan's superintendent, who also understood the importance of quick wins, was able to allocate funds to repaint the campus. It was unbelievable how much a new paint job improved the appearance and "curb-appeal" of the campus. Staff, students, and parents were very complimentary of the new colors as well as Megan's efforts in securing the resources to get this done so quickly.

Megan's staff was also concerned about safety, as there were several parts of campus where fencing was either inadequate or lacking altogether. The campus is comprised of 10 separate buildings with no interior hallways. There was no fence between the front parking lot and the buildings, which meant that anyone, at any time, could walk onto campus and into any classroom. The back playground bordered a city park. As you may know, city parks in poverty-stricken communities are often not safe places for adults, let alone children. The chain link fence that separated the school from the park was torn open in many places. There were no gates on any of the actual fence openings, which meant that, much like the front of the campus, anyone could (and did) walk onto the playground. There was a fence between the classrooms and playground, but the gates could only be locked with a chain, which was against fire code. Those gates had to stay open during the day. It wasn't uncommon for people in the community to use campus as a shortcut during the school day.

As a humorous example, Megan once received a call on her radio to come quickly to the playground because of an issue with a community member attempting to get onto the campus. She immediately left her meeting, walked briskly to the playground, and could not believe what she saw. An older gentleman, who wanted to get onto the campus as a shortcut through the community, attempted to climb over a broken section of the fence. He had lost his footing near the top of the fence and, in his free-fall to the ground, his pants got snagged. There he hung, upside down, naked.

By the second week of the summer, Megan had already begun working with the district facilities department to plan how to improve the fencing at the school. Within a few weeks, gates had been installed on all of the playground entrances, and meetings were scheduled with contractors for more major fencing and gate improvements. While the entire project took longer than a few weeks to accomplish, Megan was able to announce to the staff at one of their first staff meetings that plans were in place to address their concerns about campus safety. In her first newsletter, Megan was able to share the needed improvements with the community.

As you can see, some victories are simpler than others. Megan's perimeter fence victory took much more time and effort than my clock in the workroom. However, both had the same effect. People felt as though their opinions mattered and as though the leader had the compassion and competence to remove barriers. Yes – a clock in the workroom can be a barrier to success as foolish as that sounds.

Fix the Fixables Strategy #15: Launch (and Dissolve) Solutions Teams

Much like Carl T. Smith Middle School, Camelback High School was in a very dark place when I arrived. Much of the same issues – gangs, drugs, under-performance – were standard procedure. As I spent the summer becoming the chief historian and building relationships, I couldn't believe how many problems there were. The band had 13 students. The school had just a couple of AP courses – average enrollment under 10, average score under 2. Student achievement was the bottom of the barrel. The football team hadn't won more than one game in a season for many years. Enrollment was down 1,000 students. The list of problems went on and on.

In order to build some momentum and chip away at some of the surface level issues, I made an announcement that I would start four "ad hoc committees" or "time-bound sub-committees" that would meet for a set period of time, not ongoing. These committees, Solutions Teams, would be charged with the task of creating and implementing solutions to some of the campus' most pressing problems.

Of course, the committees that I really wanted to start weren't the ones that the campus decided upon. Had I had a choice, I would have started a team to look at teaching quality or a team to look at bell schedule changes. However, I knew that I had to first meet the needs of the staff before they could meet my needs as a leader (later). So, I left it up to the staff. They came up with the following four committees: the tardy committee, the discipline committee, the parking lot committee, and the copy center committee.

I remember thinking to myself, "Let me get this straight. After decades of under-performance, violence, and gang activity, the staff is most worried about parking and copy machines?"

At the next faculty meeting, I announced the four committees, asked for volunteers, and made a public prediction. My prediction was this – that the tardy and discipline committees would become so emotional and toxic that they'd dissolve well before they solved any issues, but that the parking lot and copy center committee would be able to create solutions to these lagging issues by fall break. Sure enough, after just one meeting each, and literally yelling and crying, both the tardy committee and the discipline committee dissolved, and the committees agreed that the campus wasn't ready to tackle such complex problems. Discipline, tardiness, and attendance are functions of culture and climate. They are not problems that can be solved by a committee. Yes, committees can create systems and structures to manage and minimize these behaviors (discipline, tardiness, attendance), but they won't eliminate the issues. I believed that then, and stand behind that still today. That doesn't mean that schools don't need strong discipline systems and structures. In fact, we'll discuss this is in detail in Chapter 10.

As predicted, the parking lot and copy center committees were successful. The parking lot committee was charged with the task of finding a solution to the "forbidden lot." The previous administration had decided that the entire front lot was only for visitors – staff was *forbidden* from parking there. The problem was this – the front lot had over 40 spots and, on average, there were 5-10 visitors parked in the lot at any given time. That meant that 30 spots – prime real estate right in front of the school – sat empty all day, in plain sight, as some teachers literally had to walk a quarter mile to their classrooms. After about four weeks, the parking lot committee rolled out a solution to the "forbidden lot" that was a great compromise between the staff wants and the community needs. Once the solution had been implemented and monitored, I dissolved the committee so that we could focus on another issue.

The second committee, the copy center committee, took a couple extra months to create a solution (that's a story for another day). Nevertheless, the proposed solution was met with great support and it resolved the issue. After a short period of time monitoring the copy center, that committee was also dissolved. Again, the purpose of these Solutions Teams are not to be permanent, problem-admiring committees like most turn out to be. These are strategic committees designed to address a specific issue, create and implement a solution, monitor for a short period of time, and then dissolve so that those individuals, and the leader, can shift time and energy to the next issue.

When Megan was reviewing the school's emergency plans, especially the fire drill and lockdown procedures, she discovered that her school's plans were in need of updating. The original plans were lacking a lot of detail and several teachers had asked relevant "what if" questions that the plans didn't answer. She quickly formed a Campus Safety committee and appointed the assistant principal to lead the process. Multiple teachers volunteered to participate and the work began immediately. Megan provided some guidance, including examples from other schools, but then let the committee do the work. Within a few weeks, not only had they drafted clear procedures for all stakeholders, they had stocked emergency backpacks to be kept in the classrooms. The committee met after the school conducted a fire drill and lockdown drill to debrief their updated procedures. Once they were satisfied with the new procedures, the committee dissolved.

Fix the Fixables Strategy #16: Focus on the Big 5

By this time, it's possible that you can't believe that a principal would spend months solving parking lot and copy center issues at a school that had fights at lunch time and terrible student achievement. On the surface, I completely agree. It sounds absolutely ridiculous that a staff cares more about copies than chemistry and that a principal would even devote time to not only listen to their concerns but also help solve them. However, over the years, I have come to realize that there are a handful of things that matter most to teachers when it comes to working climate and conditions that, if not addressed, will be constant pain points or barriers to positive climate. On the flip side, once a school masters these particular areas, teachers are happier, retention improves, and the energies typically spent on these issues can pivot to solving more important issues.

I want to now focus most of our attention on what I call the *Big 5*: parking, copies, supplies, duties, lesson plans. To put the importance of the Big 5 into perspective, consider the following brief scenarios:

> Ms. Jackson arrives to work every morning and hates where she parks, her copies aren't ready, and she doesn't have the supplies she needs to teach because the supply request process takes over a week. She is stuck doing PM duty even though she has to pick up her kids right after school, and she has to complete her lesson plans by 4:00PM on Fridays before she picks up her kids and goes home for the weekend. How happy and productive is Ms. Jackson as an employee? How likely will it be that she stays year after year?

> Mr. Gonzalez, on the other hand, arrives each morning and is happy with where he parks, his copies are ready

(or he can just hop right on a machine to make copies himself), and he has all the supplies he needs (and can even quickly grab an extra dry erase marker just in case). He has PM duty because his morning commute is over an hour, and his lesson plans are simple, electronic, and due any time before Monday morning. How happy and productive is Mr. Gonzalez as an employee? How like will it be that he stays year after year?

The great news is that making improvements to the *Big 5* is usually easy, cheap or free, and creates great goodwill and work climate. Much like the Camelback *Solutions Teams* examples above, these are also great short-term wins and perfect opportunities to engage staff in ad hoc or time-bound sub-committees.

To get you started, here is a list of questions you should consider as you think through some potential changes in these five areas:

Parking: Do you have some staff members that have to walk 10 minutes to get to their classroom? Do all of your admin have the fancy parking right in front of the school? Does drop-off and pick-up interfere with a staff member's ability to park? Do buses block staff parking spots? Are the parking gates left locked or unlocked throughout the day? Is parking lot lighting sufficient?

Copies: Do copy machines have codes that track staff member copy usage? Do you have a paper limit? Do paper jams get fixed in a timely manner? How old are the copy machines/do they work properly? Do you constantly order ink and paper so that there is no gap in service?

Supplies: Does it take an act of congress to get supplies? Does your school have an assigned supply monitor who plays favorites? Do you order the supplies your teachers really want? Is your supply room under lock and key?

Duty: Do your teachers have to do AM and PM duty? Is their duty aligned with their strengths and interests (do your more athletic teachers have cafeteria duty while your bookworms monitor the basketball courts)? Do your coaches get assigned afternoon duty that conflicts with practice? Do your early birds get PM duty and your "I need to drop my kids off every morning and may be a few minutes late" teachers get stuck with AM duty as an accountability measure? Do teachers get to pick their duties or are they assigned?

Lesson plans: Are lesson plans unreasonably long and complicated? Do the components of your lesson plan template help improve instruction? Do you read them and give consistent, helpful feedback? Do you require your highly effective teachers to complete the same plans as your new or struggling teachers?

After Megan lost her school's assistant principal position due to budget cuts, she realized that she had to make significant changes to how she led her school and how she used her resources – mainly her time and talents. Her school was rolling out weekly collaborative team meetings as part of the Professional Learning Community model it was implementing. Megan knew she had to protect her time so that she could be in every team's weekly meeting. She also knew that teachers on her campus were concerned about the increased workload (and paperwork) as a result of a new PLC model. So, Megan announced that she would no longer collect lesson plans from teachers.

Teachers were still expected to plan high-quality lessons every day, but they would not need to submit completed plans to Megan (she did remind them that, should she have concerns about a lack of quality in instruction, she would request to see their plans). Ultimately, Megan knew she would rather spend her time collaborating with teachers about instruction and being in classrooms, not reading lesson plans and emailing feedback. She also knew that she wanted her teachers spending their paperwork time on assessment data to drive instruction. This was a huge win for teachers, who felt respected and trusted as professionals.

Over the years, I have tried to convince school leaders that it's not only better for morale to have an open supply closet (or closets if your school is large enough), but that it's actually cheaper. Most don't believe me. At my middle school, supply costs went down significantly once we opened the closet (less hoarding and teachers act more like professionals when they are treated like professionals). To be honest, however, when we first opened up the closet, I thought I had made a huge mistake. Day one was a complete disaster.

The decision to open the supply wasn't taken lightly. I put a lot of thought into it. I worked with key staff members to create a system (like determining how many reams of paper the school should use each month, the approximate number of dry erase markers a teacher would need in any given week, how often to re-order supplies, etc). Susana, the school secretary, hated the idea from day one. First, she believed that teachers shouldn't and couldn't be trusted. "They're hoarders! Just go look in their closets. You won't believe all of the paper and pencils they have in there!" Second, she thought it would increase foot traffic in the office and interrupt her work. Third, and most importantly, she thought it would break the bank. She was convinced that the supply budget would have to double.

Nevertheless, I continued with the plan, communicated general expectations, talked about the supply re-order system, and set a formal date that the closet would be open. It felt like Christmas was approaching on campus. The build-up and anticipation could be felt and heard in hallways and in the parking lot. "Can you believe that next week we'll be able to get our own supplies!" was all the chatter in the workroom.

Finally, the day arrived.

For me, it was a typical Monday. I was in and out of classrooms all day. I did arrival and lunch duty. I played dodgeball with kids in PE, scarfed down a cafeteria burrito with kids in detention, and joined in Ms. Romero's art class for a while to hang out. It was about a half hour before dismissal when I finally made it back to the office for the first time that day. As soon as I arrived, Susana came to find me. I couldn't tell if she was super mad or happy. It turns out a little of both – but mainly she was in one of those "I told you so" moods.

"Mr. G. Have you been in the supply closet yet? Go look at it. You won't believe it. It's gone. It's all gone! They just took it all. No more paper. No more dry erase markers. No more pencils. They even took the pink construction paper – they don't even use pink construction paper! I told you this was a terrible idea. I don't know what we are going to do. I'll tell you one thing for sure, I'm taking that closet back. Tomorrow!"

After the lecture, I made my way back to the supply closet. My tail between my legs. Sure enough, it was nearly empty. I still have this image in my head of empty shelves and empty boxes all over the floor. Calmly, I made my way to my office. I closed the door. I drafted an email. In the subject line I simply typed, "Wow!" In the body of the email I wrote something like this.

Dear Staff –

Well, that was impressive! You managed to go through a month's worth of supplies in four hours. Nice work!

Now, I guess it shouldn't surprise me. After years of having to hoard supplies and make deals on the CTS black market to get extra dry erase markers, I probably would have done the same thing.

Part of your issue, I'm guessing, is that you aren't sure if we will actually keep the supply closet open all year. As if this is a short experiment and then we'll go back to normal. Again, I don't blame you for capitalizing on the opportunity.

First of all, I promise this is not an experiment. This is a new normal. Under no circumstances will we close the supply closet for the remainder of the year. Promise. Second, and this will be very painful for many of you, I need you all to return everything you looted out of the supply closet today. Yes, looted. I need it all returned by lunch tomorrow. I promise that I'll keep Susana away from the office so she won't bother you. And I promise to stay out of the office all morning so that the only people who witness your walk of shame are your colleagues who are doing just the same.

In the future, when you need paper, take a ream. Heck, take only a half if that's all you need. When you need a new dry erase marker, take one, not a month's supply. I trust you get it. I'll see you on Wednesday at the faculty meeting. I promise not to lecture about supplies. I may make a joke or two, but no lectures.

My best,
CG

Believe it or not, by lunch time, nearly all of the supplies had been returned. No shaming, no blaming. And, from that day forward, the staff was absolutely amazing at self-governing and self-regulating supplies. We never had to change the system or close the supply closet. And, again, we spent less on supplies after opening the closet than we did before.

Megan had a very similar supply room experience. In her second year as principal, she noticed that her secretary was often not able to get teachers the supplies they requested as quickly as needed. This wasn't out of inefficiency on the part of her secretary, but rather was due to the amount of other pressing tasks on her plate. Regardless, this caused occasional frustration for staff members which led to complaints. Megan also decided to do the unthinkable and unlock the supply room door like we did at CTS. It took a bit to convince her secretary and assistant principal, who both thought people would take advantage of this new freedom and deplete the supplies at record pace.

At her next staff meeting, she invited everyone to the lounge, where the supply room was located. There they saw a ribbon stretched across the open door and Megan had her secretary and assistant principal do the official ribbon-cutting. The staff was elated and suddenly her secretary had much more time to get other work done. They created a simple sign-out system to keep track of where supplies were going and never looked back.

There are definitely other areas (other than the *Big 5*) that matter to teachers. The quality of bathrooms and the quality of lunch options in the cafeteria are two others that impact climate. Teachers and staff also care about the number of daily interruptions that occur over the intercom system, how long their lunch is, how long their prep period is and how often it is taken from them, when (during the day) their prep period lands, and what subjects or grade levels they teach. These, and other, are areas that you and your staff can explore as you work to improve working conditions. Remember – teacher and staff working conditions are your students' learning conditions.

Fix the Fixables Strategy #17: Have Fun with Your Staff

Making sure teachers get their copies done on time and making improvements to the duty schedule is a great way to start improving campus climate and the working environment. Removing barriers to getting supplies, demonstrating that you care by asking about an anniversary, and solving simple day-to-day problems can be such a morale booster for teachers and staff. Often, these basic daily issues, if left unresolved, can chip away at climate and culture and have such a dramatic impact on the environment. That's why the *Big 5* and other common areas of concern are a perfect place for a leader to start. But that's just a start. It's also important to create opportunities for the adults on your campus to have fun, interact with each other, and build relationships with colleagues. Yes, teachers and staff, even in this cut-throat, accountability-driven, every-minute-counts era can and should have fun at work.

If you are like me, you may be terrible at creating and planning fun activities. I always have been and always will be. A decade ago, I "organized" a huge 30th birthday party for Megan. To me, "organized" meant inviting her friends and ordering food. That evening when everyone showed up, Megan's friend came to find me about an hour into the gathering. "So, what's the plan for the night?"

"Plan? What do you mean, plan?" I said.

"You know, like a game or an activity. Perhaps a roast? Maybe dessert and some story telling? You have a cake, right?" she inquired.

I had gotten everyone to the party and ordered the food, but I didn't do anything else. No dessert. No games. No candles. No activities. No fun. That is pretty much me at work. I know that team-building and fun is extremely important – I am just not good at planning or executing it. The great news is, there are many people that love this stuff.

They love making invitations, planning activities, and coordinating events. If you aren't good at it, delegate this to someone or to a team. I always had a "Fluff Committee" that I created to take the lead on fun. Yes, I literally called it the Fluff Committee. Whether it's you, someone else, or a committee, being intentional about having fun as a staff is a necessary component of improving climate and working conditions. Again, removing barriers was just the beginning. Below, I have made a list of activities and events that both Megan and I have used over the years to build a stronger sense of team, family, community:

> **Underground Spirit Day:** Organize a day, without students knowing, when all of the staff dress up the same way – college day, beach day, wear red day, etc.

> **Bagel and Donut Fridays:** It doesn't cost that much money to buy 50 to 100 donuts and bagels once a month to just thank your staff for a great week.

> **Pancake Feed:** One of my favorite mornings at CTS was our quarterly pancake feed. My mother-in-law bought me a pancake grill that I left in the workroom. Quarterly, I would buy pancake batter, syrup, fruit, and whipping cream. Then, that morning in the workroom, I would put on an apron and spend the morning cooking pancakes for the staff.

> **Ice Cream Socials:** Much like bagels and donuts, it doesn't cost much money at all to buy 50 to 100 popsicles or ice cream sandwiches to hand out after school one day.

> **Cancel a Staff Meeting:** Sometimes the best thing you can do as a school leader is cancel a staff meeting and

encourage people to get caught up on work and even sneak out early.

Staff Olympics: Some of the best days we ever had as a staff at CTS was Staff Olympics. We'd pick 5-6 events (free throws, Pictionary ™, chess, Jeopardy ™, etc.). Then each grade level would assign members of its team to the event they thought would have the best chance at winning. Winners would get one point. 2nd place would get two points. 3rd place would get three points. Teams that got 4th place or worse would get four points. At the end of the Olympics, the team with the lowest score would win.

Amazing Race: On a couple of occasions, I have organized an Amazing Race ™ competition to start the school year. Instead of starting the first faculty meeting of the year with reviewing data and setting goals (which we'd do later), we would begin with an Amazing Race. Teams would have to complete a series of tasks, find locations, and solve riddles. At the end of each task or activity, teams would have to take a picture of themselves to prove they completed it. They'd send pictures to one email account and, throughout the race, someone on the staff would compile a slideshow that we'd show when the race ended. The first team to finish the race would be the winners. Tasks would range from building bridges out of marshmallows and toothpicks to finding the best place for students to make-out on campus to picking up a "to go" menu from their favorite lunch spot.

Flash mobs: Although this may be out of fashion by now, one of the most enjoyable team-building activities I have ever been a part of was the time the staff at

Camelback secretly memorized a dance and then, one day right at dismissal, surprised the students with a staff flash mob.

Lip Syncing: As Megan began her fourth year, she knew she needed to take team-building to a new level with her staff. So, on the first morning of their summer in-service week, she announced that they would have a Lip Sync Battle. She started it off by showing a quick clip of a popular TV show and then assigned each staff member to a team. She made sure to put people together who typically didn't work together, like the kindergarten teacher and junior high social studies teacher. Megan knew she had a few who would be completely uncomfortable with this activity, so she made them the judges.
Teams had a list of suggested songs to choose from and 30 minutes to prepare their performance. They would be scored on accuracy, use of props, choreography, and overall entertainment. The results were hilarious, to say the least. Not only did this activity give people a chance to work with new people in a fun, non-work sort of way, but it also revealed a lot of hidden talent and humor in the staff. Two of the shyest teachers on staff were the biggest stars – one as a hula dancer and one as the iceberg from The Titanic.

Celebrity: In preparing for an upcoming staff meeting, Megan realized that the staff was in need of a good laugh and a break from professional development. After a few housekeeping items, she reviewed the objectives for the staff meeting. They read something like this:

1. Staff will use descriptive language to identify

characters from various literature, politics, and entertainment.

2. Staff will identify the most important details to describe characters from various literature, politics, and entertainment.

3. Staff will use non-verbal cues to describe characters from various literature, politics, and entertainments.

The staff was completely baffled until Megan announced that they would be playing the popular party game, Celebrity. They spent the next hour laughing, shouting, and gesturing. They quickly found out who were closet-competitors and who knew a little too much about 90's pop culture.

Pranks: Below we'll share two pranks that were pulled against us – one against me, the other against Megan. Of course, you have to be very careful with pranks, as some people have more tolerance for pranks than others. However, pranks can be a very fun way to bring the staff together.

On the second to last day of school one year, Megan's staff played an epic prank on her. While Megan was scrambling around getting ready for the 8th grade promotion ceremony, teachers, parents, and even a few students snuck outside to cover her entire car in sticky notes. Some of them had messages, like "I already signed my contract" and "#don'tfireus." They even found tooth-shaped notes from a dentist's office to put on the car's front grill.

Megan didn't notice until she was leading the 8th graders on a final "walk" around campus before they went into their promotion ceremony. After taking a few pictures, she and some helpful students went about the task of taking off all the notes. The only problem was this all happened at the end of May in Phoenix in extreme heat. The sticky notes had a few hours to cook onto her car and it took roughly 4 trips through the car wash in order to get the residue off.

Perhaps the most memorable community-building activity I've been involved in was the day that the staff at CTS decided to organize a well-thought-out and well-orchestrated prank against me. They pulled off more than one, but this was their best. It was the end of the year, and I had just handed out that dreaded "End of Year Check Out" form. You know – that list that principals deliver to teachers and staff with a couple weeks left to go that tells them that they won't get their summer paychecks if they don't turn in their grades, their keys, and their textbooks.

The staff got together the evening that I handed out the check-out form and decided to create one for me. They went to the store, bought a chain and lock, and actually chained my door closed so that I couldn't open it. I had to complete ten tasks on an End of Year Check Out form before someone would unlock my door for me. Although the list was way out of my comfort zone, I decided to play along. Throughout the day, among other tasks, I had to do an interpretive dance in the art room, perform the Napoleon Dynamite dance on the stage during lunch, deliver lemons to the PE teacher (inside joke), and dress up like a student (our students had to wear uniforms). It took me a few hours, but I eventually got my office back. Although it's been over a decade, I still have that chain and lock.

Fix the Fixables Strategy #18: Be Patient

Perhaps the most difficult part of *Build Relationships*, *Enhance Your Institutional Knowledge*, and *Fix the Fixables* is being patient and not creating too much change. Remember, people want you to fix their problems, not create change. Most people are change-adverse. They like stability and predictability. Leaders, on the other hand, love change. They love to identify problems and change systems and structures. They love experimenting and risk-taking. They love implementing bold and audacious ideas. There is obviously a sharp contrast here, which is why there is often such tension between a new leader and his or her staff.

This is why this fifth strategy is so important. A leader must be disciplined. She or he must be strategic and intentional about nearly every action and reaction. As mentioned before, new leaders who take time to relationship build and ask questions will find a thousand things wrong with any given school. The natural tendency of a leader is to fix and change all of those things as soon as possible. That's detrimental. Organizations (and people) can only handle so much change at a time. You, the leader, don't have the bandwidth or hours in a day to fix everything that's broken and solve every problem. Megan's first year at Norma Jones is a perfect example of this.

As Megan worked through her first year as principal, she constantly discovered issues and challenges that needed to be addressed. It wasn't long before she was completely overwhelmed and discouraged, feeling like she needed to fix everything immediately. She knew it was unrealistic to think she could (and should) resolve everything in one year. She was also lucky enough to have a superintendent who understood the change process and didn't expect a complete turnaround in one year. Nevertheless, she continued to stress herself out trying to figure out how she would get it all done.

During one of our conversations about her ongoing leadership dilemmas, I convinced Megan to set just two or three goals for herself and her school for the remainder of the school year – no more, no less. After making a list of everything that she was losing sleep over, we talked through which items would have the most significant and meaningful impact on her staff and students. From that, she created three goals to accomplish by the end of the school year:

1. Develop a strong leadership structure and vision statement for the school

2. Establish school-wide behavior expectations and a system for holding students accountable to those expectations

3. Focus on 1-2 "problem" employees that were no longer a good fit for the school

From that point on, despite the pull to do more, she prioritized these three reasonable and attainable goals and forced herself to pause, not abandon, the other items on the list. She also worked with her leadership teams to determine a 3-year plan for addressing the other issues at the right time. In leadership team meetings, they often used the phrase "that's year 2" or "that's year 3" to help pace themselves while still recognizing the importance of the issues.

The moral of the story: be patient. Even if when you want to go fast, slow down. If you go too fast, you'll get a speeding ticket. As a colleague used to tell me, "sometimes you have to go slow to go fast." Leadership is a marathon, not a sprint. Pace yourself. This will pay dividends for you in the long run.

Chapter 8
<u>O</u>rganize Leadership, Learning, and Listening Structures
Establish teams and structures that enhance inclusivity and collaboration to broaden voice and perspective as well as increase motivation and empowerment

The book *Trusting Teachers with School Success* asks, "What would teachers do if they had the autonomy to not just make classroom decisions, but to collectively – with their colleagues – make the decisions influencing whole school success?" This particular book, *Trusting Teachers*, and many others like it that promote teacher-run schools, base much of their research and theories on the idea of shared or distributive leadership. Ritchie and Woods (2007) describe distributive leadership as "distributing responsibility on all administrative levels, working through teams, and engendering collective responsibility." Natsiopoulou and Giouroukakis (2010) suggest that distributed, and even democratic, leadership "promotes the staff's full participation in key decision-making and implementation processes and also makes them accountable."

For what it's worth, I'm not advocating for teacher-run schools. However, BTL is closely aligned with the fundamental beliefs of the teacher-run schools movement – namely, that schools operate more effectively with leadership *distributed* as much and as often as possible to those who work in the trenches. Leaders must understand that effective school leadership today, unlike in decades past, is highly inclusive and collaborative, and that collective wisdom and collective effort improves outcomes for staff and students and expedites the change process.

Less effective, top-down leaders who don't subscribe to shared leadership find themselves constantly seeking *buy-in*. *Buy-in* is the lowest form of engagement and often leads to reluctant compliance. Compliance-based leadership is not leadership. That's management. Moderately effective leaders who understand that autocratic leadership is a practice of the past, yet don't fully believe in collective leadership, operate under the assumption that *empowerment* is the gold standard of leadership. Granted, empowerment surely produces a higher level of engagement than *buy-in*; however, simply delegating authority to staff to lead initiatives is still a very low-level form of distributive leadership. What truly transformative leaders seek is *co-ownership*. Not *buy-in*. Not *empowerment*. *Ownership*. When key stakeholders *own* vision, values, and initiatives just as much as the leader does, commitment increases exponentially and change is sustainable far beyond the tenure of the leader. Ultimately, the mark of a true leader is the impact she or he has well beyond the time at any given organization.

One of the only problems with collaborative, distributive, or democratic leadership in schools in particular is that principals often only include their teachers in the decision-making process. Leaders often forget that the entire orchestra of stakeholders has important insight and can offer different talents and resources that teachers can't. Maintenance workers are best equipped to solve maintenance problems. Cafeteria workers should help inform changes in cafeteria procedures. Teachers should engage intimately in decisions impacting teaching and learning. Playground aides should be the primary voice in modifying playground rules. Likewise, students, parents, and the greater community – neighbors, business leaders, local community groups – can also add great value to decision-making. As such, these other key stakeholders can and should play a large role in advising school leaders and even assisting with implementation of new ideas or initiatives when possible. In this chapter, we'll explore four different leadership structures that a principal should consider when sharing leadership responsibilities, all aimed at increasing ownership and making better informed decisions.

Before moving on, it's important to note why this chapter is titled *Organize Leadership, Learning, and Listening Structures* and not just *Organize Leadership Structures*. Of course, leadership teams and advisory groups do exist to help leaders more effectively and efficiently share or distribute leadership for the many reasons mentioned above – collective capacity, ownership, sustainable change. But these teams and groups exist for two other important reasons.

The first is learning. I once had a superintendent mentor who named his executive team the *Learning Leadership Team*. He said that all three of those characteristics mattered – learning, leadership, team. He said that without any of those characteristics, the team would lack purpose, vision, effectiveness, cohesiveness. He also said that he purposefully put *learning* first in the title because teams that learn together grow together and stay together. "Teams that don't, don't" he told me. As you'll see in the next chapter, learning together is an essential step in the change process.

The second is listening. In Chapter 6, we shared a Strategy titled, *In All Your Firsts, Listen More Than You Speak*. One of the greatest tools a leader has in his or her toolbox is the ability to listen. This is true not only for a leader's "firsts" but also throughout a leader's entire leadership career. Unfortunately, leaders believe that, especially in leadership teams and community meetings, the leader must do most of the talking. That's simply not true. Leadership teams, advisory groups, and community meetings should be opportunities to listen and learn just as much as they are to lead.

By my fourth year at Camelback, I decided that my Mondays would be dedicated entirely to leading, learning, and listening. Monday tended to be the most predictable day of the week – other than managing any weekend crises, Monday behavior of staff and students always seemed to be at its best. It was a day that required great stamina for me – 9 straight structured hours that did not include catching up on email or other paperwork. When you see the schedule below, you'll assume it was an exhausting day of talking, leading, and decision-making. However, the day was built intentionally to be a day that had a perfect blend of leading, learning, and listening. Here is a copy of my Monday schedule, starting at 7:30AM.

7:30-8:00AM – *Lead Tutor Meeting**
*Camelback eventually developed a comprehensive tutoring program called Success Is Mandatory (more information at www.SuccessIsMandatory.com) that was run by students – lead tutors – who tracked data, led tutoring sessions, and made adjustments to programming on a weekly basis with my input. Every Monday morning I met with them in my office.

8:00-8:20AM – *Monday Morning Line Up**
*I held a standing (literally, standing) meeting with security staff, office staff, and various other staff members every Monday to review the major events of the week, share celebrations or concerns, and debrief the previous week's (and weekend's) activities. This idea was borrowed from the Ritz Carlton ™ Daily Line Up expectation that all leaders must hold a brief, standing daily meeting to review the list of special guests and events occurring that day in the hotel.

8:30-10:30AM – Weekly Admin Meeting (I had 4 assistant principals)

10:30-11:00AM – *Daily Meeting** with secretary

Both Megan and I, having gone through The Breakthrough Coach ™ training, always hold daily meetings with our secretaries to review calendars, mail, paperwork, voicemail, and so on.

11:00-11:30AM – Meet with student leaders from *Montessori College Prep**
　　*An autonomous school-within-a-school at Camelback that we launched in 2013

11:30-12:15PM – Hang out with staff and students during 1ˢᵗ lunch (and eat lunch *on the go***)**

12:15-1:00PM – Attend *Student Government* **class**

1:00-1:30PM – Meet with student representatives from *Camelback Virtual**
　　　　*Typically classes taken by students who were credit-deficient or had unsatisfactory attendance

1:30-2:00PM – Classroom walk-throughs

2:00-3:15PM – *Instructional Cabinet*

3:15-4:30PM – *Organizational Cabinet*

It took me four years at Camelback to evolve into this schedule. First-year principals don't need to begin their leadership careers this way – it takes time to develop systems and structures for leading, learning, and listening like this. Some may even argue that, even after four years, this is too much for one day. Regardless of your reaction, this schedule was highly intentional. I was able to have touch points with nearly every major decision-maker and influencer on campus every Monday. It ensured that I had a strong, accurate pulse on campus climate and was able to make small adjustments or even improve communication with the entire school community based on the feedback. As you see, I ended the day with two *Cabinets* – Instructional and Organizational. For this chapter's specific *Strategies*, we'll begin there.

<u>O</u>rganize Leadership, Learning, and Listening Structures
Strategy #19: A Two-Team Approach

Many leaders today, when asked how they distribute or share leadership on their campuses, point to their academic leadership team. In elementary schools, this is often a team made up of grade level representatives. In middle school and high school, this may be a combination of grade level reps and department chairs. This team, often hand-selected by principals or through some sort of formalized process, is charged with the task of making most of the major decisions on the campus – from grading to bell schedules to curricular changes to dismissal duties to parent-teacher conference dates.

What I've found in my leadership journey is that this one-team approach to shared leadership is a flawed leadership structure, and it's flawed for three reasons. First, one team should not be responsible for making all academic *and* non-academic decisions. This is too big of a task for one small group of leaders, especially on large campuses. Second, more often than not, this one team is made up of teachers only. Teachers, though the anchor staff on any given campus, have a narrow perspective and often aren't the best staff members to recommend non-academic improvements such as managing visitors to campus or supervising the weight room after school. Finally, to make matters worse, this one team is often made up of teachers that the rest of the staff would consider to be the "favorites" of the principal. The result can very easily become limited buy-in on any new program, initiative, or mandate that originates from this team.

As an alternative to this model, I believe strongly that all campuses should use a two-team approach to leadership – one team that focuses on all things academic and another that focuses on all things non-academic. These teams should also have very different selection and participation processes. More on that in a moment.

Ultimately, it does not matter what these teams are called. While I was at CTS, I called one team the Academic Leadership Team and the other the Site Leadership Team. At Camelback, I titled one Instructional Cabinet and the other Organizational Cabinet. At Norma Jones, Megan calls one Vision Cabinet and the other Mission Cabinet. Again, the names don't matter but the purpose(s) should. These two teams play a critical role in the change process on a campus. In the next chapter, we'll explore some specific actions and activities that these teams should engage in when considering major changes. For now, let's take a deeper look into this two-team approach.

Academic Leadership Team

In general, the academic team should be a select group of effective, exemplary educators. They should be selected by site administration, or by a formalized process that enables peers to select who they believe is the most effective leader in any given area (whether that's fourth grade in elementary or the science department in middle school or high school). Most often, this team is made up of respected grade level reps and department chairs. Regardless of the formal make-up or the selection process, this team must consist of highly competent teachers who not only have a proven track record of strong academic gains but are also willing to help spread proven practices (and, therefore, those results) to other classrooms. Finally, this team, more specifically, should be responsible for leading teaching, learning, curriculum, supplemental materials, assessment, interventions, enrichment, and professional development.

Non-Academic Leadership Team

Generally speaking, this non-academic team should look and feel very different than the academic team. First, I strongly encourage you to have your 1-2 most dedicated and influential teacher leaders on campus serve on both teams – they can then serve as communicators and liaisons between the two teams. Second, this team must include more than teachers and should consist of a variety of key classified and certified staff members, from counselors to custodians to cafeteria staff to crossing guards.

Finally, consider opening up participation on this team to anyone on campus who wants to engage productively. I know that, to most leaders, this may be a radical shift from past practice. However, opening up membership or participation to any and all does three things: (a) removes any accusations that leadership teams on campus are only for the principal's favorites; (b) gives an opportunity for non-traditional leaders to join, including those textbook introverts who don't typically say "pick me"; and (c) it allows the leader to develop more leaders (and more supporters) in more areas of the campus that are traditionally not listened to or even forgotten. The primary functions or focus areas of a non-academic cabinet include, but are not limited to:

> Student discipline (from tardy policies to after-school detention to Saturday School)
>
> Culture, climate, and community activities (open houses, field days, assemblies, and parent events)
>
> Four of the *Big 5* (copies, supplies, parking, duties – lesson plans are the responsibility of the academic

leadership team)

Dismissal and arrival issues (bus loading zones, late parents, etc.)

Recess (schedule, supplies, coverage, etc.)

As you can see from these lists, there is so much work to be done, so many decisions to be made, and so many areas to oversee within a school that putting all of this burden on one academic leadership team is not wise. In fact, when academic leadership teams are also responsible for areas like discipline and open houses, they often put academics on the backburner, negatively impacting student achievement. Conversely, having two teams tackle all major campus issues allows a leader to distribute the work more efficiently and effectively. In many ways, it doubles the capacity of the campus to address problems, implement solutions, and drive change.

When I arrived at Camelback in 2009, the campus subscribed to the typical one-team approach. In Camelback's case, this team was titled Instructional Cabinet. This team, although it consisted of some of the most respected and effective teachers on campus, wasn't functioning well. In one meeting, this team would argue about tardiness and absences, then shift to problems with the testing schedule and student placement, and then end the meeting complaining about the copy center. After observing and even leading Instructional Cabinet for a couple weeks, I decided to launch an Organizational Cabinet. I did not disband Instructional Cabinet – I simply narrowed their focus to all things teaching and learning. This team began to focus on major campus initiatives that impacted classrooms – PLCs, evaluations, master schedule/student placement, and so forth. Over the years, because of the narrower focus, Instructional Cabinet became a highly effective team that produced amazing results for staff and students.

In late-August of that first year, I publicly opened up membership to Organizational Cabinet but released, in essence, a job description so that "Org Cabinet" was made up of the right people with the right intent. The description was as follows:

> Must be fully committed to the success of Camelback – staff, students, community
>
> Must be willing to attend meetings every week, after school, unpaid, on Tuesdays (and perhaps even on weekends, if needed)
>
> Must be willing to be a positive, productive contributor
>
> Must be willing to engage in sub-committees, if needed, outside of formal Organizational Cabinet meetings
>
> Must be willing to be a leader and an influencer

If staff members felt they met this criteria and wanted to join, they were in. There was no vetting process and no rubric. Simply, people were asked to self-assess to determine whether or not they fit. On the first day of Organizational Cabinet, nearly 75 people showed up. I knew at that point that, as bad as things were at Camelback at the time, the future was bright if 75 people felt they met that criteria. In the next chapter, I will share some of the journey of this particular team, how it functioned, and what it accomplished.

Early on in her first year as principal, Megan developed a leadership structure that would involve several staff members and give equal attention to the academic and non-academic needs of her school. She created a "cabinet," or leadership team, for teaching and learning, and a cabinet for operations, culture, and climate. For the first two years, Megan and her team constantly reflected, revised, and renamed the structures as they grew and changed. They eventually settled on a Mission Cabinet and a Vision Cabinet.

Members of the Mission Cabinet are all *Collaborative Team Leaders* on campus, along with the *instructional coach* and one of the special education teachers. The school had embarked on becoming a *Professional Learning Community* and this team is responsible for monitoring the academic goals, along with planning and implementing school-wide strategies for collaboration and instructional improvement. Essentially, they were in charge of making sure the school was following through on their academic mission to "inspire, challenge, and ensure that everyone learns and succeeds at their highest potential."

The Vision Cabinet, in turn, focused on "living" the school's vision of being "a community of high school-ready and college and career-bound learners, leaders, and achievers." They identified 6 pillars of their vision – Community, High School-Readiness, College and Career, Learners, Leaders, and Achievers. For each of the 5 pillars (Learners was exempt as it was already being owned by the Mission Cabinet), they formed a committee. Every staff member joined a committee, with the Vision Cabinet members serving as committee leads. Each committee developed, planned, and implemented initiatives aligned with their respective pillars. For example, the Leaders committee started a Student Ambassador program and the Achievers committee planned out student recognition nights throughout the year. The Vision Cabinet also monitored the school's behavior goals and helped monitor the school-wide expectations and accountability plan.

Not only did this leadership structure take a lot of weight off Megan's shoulders, but it allowed many staff members to step up into leadership roles – distributing leadership among virtually every staff member. In addition, staff investment (*ownership*) in the school was heightened, and they were able to trust that the work they were doing was aligned to a bigger idea that they helped develop. Ultimately, the greatest outcome was student success. With the staff organized and focused, they were able to confidently provide a safe, innovative, and supportive learning experience for students that focused on their success today and tomorrow.

The final recommendation related to this two-team approach is to be intentional about bringing these two groups together a few times per year. There is no magic number – just be sure to have these two teams meet on a calendared-basis. For both Megan and me, these teams met quarterly or, minimally, semesterly with a summer retreat in between. It is important that these teams stay connected to each, support and complement (and not contradict or conflict) each other, and help drive each other's work. For example, when the academic leadership decides the school should have academic achievement assemblies, not just sports pep rallies, the non-academic team should help calendar and coordinate the assemblies. In the same light, if the non-academic team wants to distribute a culture/climate survey, the academic leadership team should help determine how and when to have students take the survey to minimize the loss of instructional time. The point, of course, is that the two teams must have a strong enough relationship to help support, not oppose, each other's activities and initiatives.

Organize Leadership, Learning, and Listening Structures
Strategy #20: Student Advisory Groups

If you recall my Monday schedule, there were multiple opportunities throughout the day for me to meet and interact with students – in some cases very informally and in others more formally. Either way, the goal of this strategy – *Student Advisory Groups* - is to create time and space to engage consistently and meaningfully with students to build relationships, seek feedback, and, ultimately, make changes and improvements to the school using student voice.

As you have probably seen throughout your own career in education, there are many ways in which principals seek feedback from students. There is no one right way. Many principals across the country establish specific groups or councils just for this purpose – the "Principal's Student Advisory Council" or the "Principal's Student Leadership Team." Other principals plug into existing structures such as weekly or monthly meetings with Student Council. There is also no research that details how often or how frequently a leader should seek feedback from students – it's a matter of time and capacity for each leader.

Regardless of which approach you use – creating your own team or using an existing student group – there are a few key factors to keep in mind. First, it is important that if you are going to seek feedback, you use it. Nothing hurts climate and morale more than a leader who appears to listen and care, and makes promises, but never delivers. If your female students say that they need tampon or pad dispensers in the girls bathrooms, you better deliver. If your students say that the biggest issue with cheeseburger day in the cafeteria is that there is no mustard, you better go shopping. If your students say that they need new basketball nets on the outside courts, you pull out the ladder and install them yourself if you have to. (By the way, these are real examples that have occurred throughout my tenure).

Second, it is extremely important that you seek feedback on what's working **and** on what's not working. Some leaders find themselves always looking for one or the other. Some want to only hear the good to make themselves feel better. Others look for the bad so that they can lecture their staff about what they aren't doing right. Truth is, leaders need to hear both. They need to hear the good so that they can publicly celebrate what's working and recognize those responsible for the success. They also need to hear the bad so that they know what to improve or change.

Finally, when engaging with students, don't fall into the trap that the vast majority of other leaders fall into – don't only meet with high performing, well-behaved, and highly-active students. It is critical that you meet with students in the middle, students who are struggling, students who are disruptive. The primary reason that I met with Camelback Virtual students every Monday is because these were largely the unsuccessful and disenfranchised students at the school. As leaders make changes to improve outcomes for students, it is critically important for them to know what *all* students believe and experience – not just the high fliers.

One of the greatest examples of this occurred during my first year at Camelback. Our Organizational Cabinet had made a decision to launch an Advisory program and was in the design phase. At first, the staff felt strongly that a one-day per week Advisory period was the best place to start. A one-day Advisory would give faculty just enough time to build relationships with students, have a set weekly check-in, monitor grades and attendance, and connect students with needed resources (counseling, after-school tutoring, etc.). Once the team had created the framework for Advisory, I began to meet with students to get feedback. I met with Student Government, Honor Society, and DECA to get their insight. They loved the idea and were excited to have an opportunity to connect more consistently with an "advisor" (a teacher) who could help guide them through high school. I also met with our AVID students – those in the middle – and they were equally supportive. So, based on their feedback, we continued as planned with the one-day Advisory period.

I then decided to do something untraditional. Camelback still had gang issues on campus at that time. These gangs didn't necessarily cause issues day-to-day but they were at the center of most of the fights, drugs, and graffiti issues on campus when they did occur. I decided that I wanted to meet with one particular gang, so I tried to approach them one day at lunch. At the sight of the principal coming, they quickly dispersed. One of the security staff on campus, Dan, saw the failed attempt and approached me to see if he could help. I explained what I was trying to do, and Dan told me he could arrange for a meeting behind closed doors. He said there was no way these boys could be seen talking with the principal in public.

A couple of days later, Dan brought Manuel and a couple of his friends to my office. The boys assumed they were in trouble or were about to be interrogated, even though they were assured by Dan that wasn't the case. Ahead of time, I had the boys' transcripts printed so that I could review their academic records with them. None were on track to graduate. The leader, Manuel, was the closest to being "on track" but had failed the state exam three times in a row. His scores *fell far below* the standard and the state exam was, at the time in Arizona, a graduation requirement.

I decided that first meeting to just relationship-build and talk about their transcripts. Although it was obvious the others had no interest in their academic progress, Manuel showed some interest. He sat up in his chair when he learned that he was just two classes behind and, if he could take two night school classes online, he would only have the state exam to worry about. He said that no one in his family had ever graduated from high school and that it would be "cool" to be the first. The meeting ended there – on a positive note. Manuel agreed to come back down in a couple days to see me. He even said he would meet without Dan present. He said that his "brothers" wouldn't be joining us next time.

Over the next couple of weeks, Manuel and I developed a relationship behind closed doors. Manuel officially agreed to take two evening school online classes, and I promised to provide him all the support he needed to pass the state exam. During one of the meetings, I shared the general details of the Advisory program we were developing. Manuel thought, much like graduation, that Advisory would be "cool" but said that for students like him it would be important that the right teachers were placed with the right students. "You know, some teachers just aren't as cool as others," he said.

When I explained that Advisory would be just one period per week, Manuel asked, "Why would you only do one day per week? Why not all five?"

"Well." I thought for a moment. "I guess we thought that one day per week would be the right first step."

"What about students like me who could use that time to get AIMS tutoring? Maybe I could pass my test if I could get tutoring during the day. I might even get more of my homework done if we could get extra time? I don't do homework at home."

The conversation about Advisory continued for another 10 minutes. I asked a few more probing questions to get some of his ideas on paper. I then took that information back to Organizational Cabinet. The team then spent the next few weeks grappling with the pros and cons of an all-week Advisory period – there were plenty of both. After getting feedback from the staff, the team began to design a five-day per week Advisory program to see if it would even be possible – politically and practically. Eventually, after months of planning and communication, we implemented Advisory – five days per week. If it wasn't for the conversation with Manuel, this would never have happened.

To get you started, I have made a list of ways that principals can create time and space to lead, learn from, and listen to students.

1) **Student Council/Government:** This is arguably the most natural and easiest place for a leader to engage. "StuCo" or "StuGo" is typically a group of students – largely extroverts – already looking to have more voice and not afraid to share the good, the bad, and the ugly with campus administration.

2) **Principal's Honor Roll:** If you have not already begun an Honor Roll in your school, I'll do my best to convince you of this in Chapter 10. For now, just know that Honor Roll is not only a great way to recognize your best students but also a way for a leader to get valuable insight from the school's best and brightest.

3) **Student of the Month (or Quarter):** Launching a Student of the Month program, if your school doesn't already have one, has three clear benefits: (1) much like Honor Roll, it gives a school leader another group to connect with, (2) also like Honor Roll, it is a way to recognize students who are displaying the attitudes and behaviors you want other students to emulate, and (3) unlike Honor Roll, Student of the Month programs allow teachers and school leaders to celebrate students who, although they may not be your typical Honor Roll student, are showing significant improvement or are in need of public recognition to help them through challenging personal times.

4) **Selective Programs:** Most middle schools and high schools already have classes, clubs, and programs like Honor Societies, DECA, or FBLA that attract successful students who are willing to share insight and perspective to school leaders to make sure that the school has the right level of rigor and support for high achieving students.

5) **Lunch Detention, After-School Detention, or ISS:** It is critical that school leaders don't only associate with the "best and brightest," so to speak. It may not always be the best idea, or even an option, to meet with a gang leader like I did, but there are other structures and systems on campus – like detention or in-school

suspension – that a leader can attend or pull students from to seek feedback.

6) **United Nations:** This suggestion is largely for high schools, although some middle schools are able to offer an array of clubs and sports. While I was at Camelback, all of the club presidents and sports captains convened once a quarter – this was called *United Nations*. They discussed and even jointly planned major school events like Homecoming, Hoopcoming, and Open Houses. This is was always a convenient way for me to get in front of my most influential students to share ideas as well as get input.

7) **House of Representatives:** After we established the Advisory program at Camelback, we created a new student leadership structure – House of Representatives. The idea was simple – each Advisory class chose a representative to participate in quarterly meetings with the principal. The primary objective was originally to seek input on how to improve and strengthen Advisory. Eventually, the group began to look at other important school-wide issues.

<u>O</u>rganize Leadership, Learning, and Listening Structures
Strategy #21: Parent Advisory Council

During the first week of my time at Carl T. Smith, I wanted to make sure that I met as many parents as possible. So instead of organizing the typical *Meet the Teacher* night, we decided to offer eight (yes, eight) *Meet the Principal* meetings with the goal of getting 100% parent participation by the end of the first week. We offered three before school/breakfast meetings, one lunch meeting, and four evening meetings that week. Although we never quite reached 100% attendance, we did get close. More importantly, my staff and I were able to meet nearly every parent in a smaller group setting, establish new expectations, ask and answer questions, and get feedback. We were then armed with new *intelligence* that we used when making decisions about changes in the future.

At Camelback, I inherited a very broken and poorly attended Parent Teacher Association, or PTA. After just a few meetings, because the meetings were terribly unproductive, I decided to shut down the PTA, take a few months off, and then re-launch a new structure for seeking parent feedback when the timing was right.

Eventually, when the timing was right, I launched a smaller parent group that I simply titled, Parent Advisory Council (PAC). The PAC met with me once per quarter for an early evening dinner meeting – our culinary students prepared and served the food. The group had only 10-12 members on the team so that the group wouldn't get too large – too many people, too many opinions. I made sure that the parents represented different factions of the school. There were freshman, sophomore, junior, and senior parents. There were parents of athletes and bookworms. There were parents of Honor Society students as well as struggling students. There were loud parents and quiet parents. And, of course, the parents themselves were representative of the overall demographics of the school.

The team was not responsible for fundraising or parent communication – instead, the team served as another vehicle to seek feedback and get advice. We discussed campus climate issues. I shared teaching and learning progress. We brainstormed ways in which to better engage parents. I gave them previews into major changes on the horizon and asked for honest and even critical feedback. Members of the PAC were free to add their own items to agenda, which they often did. They often wanted to talk about rumors about a varsity coach that was too tough on his kids, a teacher who was failing too many students, after school issues at the local park, or, conversely, a security guard that the students loved who should be recognized.

This parent group became a support group for me. I grew to love them, and they me. When I needed parents to spread the word about a new change, such as a new bell schedule, they were right there behind me. When I made a varsity coaching change that upset some parents, they were there to back me. If I needed parent volunteers for an event, they were the first to volunteer. In many ways, they became much more than an advisory council, they became another leadership team that helped drive and navigate change.

Of course, promoting a smaller parent council does not mean that I am not a proponent of formalized PTAs or PTOs. In fact, quite the opposite. Strong, vibrant parent groups can be transformative for school communities. Through PTAs and PTOs, schools can improve parent communication and parent participation. Schools can often launch major fundraisers, campaigns, and initiatives through large, more formalized PTAs and PTOs. Any official parent group that already exists on a campus, provided it is a functional group that was formed for the right reasons and right purpose (helping the school, not furthering an agenda), should be leveraged as much as possible to improve outreach and engagement.

As a leader, if you arrive to a campus that doesn't have a formalized parent group, and you don't feel as though you have the bandwidth to launch a new parent group at the moment, one of the easiest places to start is with a *Coffee with the Principal* program.

Megan's school had a parent center that consistently had 5-10 parents inside, mainly accessing Rosetta Stone to learn English or enjoying each other's company. After noticing the school did not have any structures in place for the principal to engage regularly with families, Megan began hosting monthly *Coffee with the Principal* meetings. Held the first Tuesday of every month, these informal meetings allowed Megan to sit down with parents, share successes and upcoming events, and get parent input and feedback on school and district plans. On occasion, guest speakers would come and present, but more often than not, it was a casual conversation with no agenda.

Megan set some boundaries, such as not bringing up concerns specific just to their child(ren), or making complaints about staff. She reminded parents that they are always welcome to meet with her privately to discuss any concerns of that nature, but wanted the coffee meetings to be ones that were productive and relevant to all in attendance. It didn't take long for parents to feel comfortable with being honest and asking important questions, and Megan gained tremendous insight from the discussions. She was able to share the outcomes and/or summarize the conversation, for better or worse, with her staff the very next day during monthly staff meetings.

<u>O</u>rganize Leadership, Learning, and Listening Structures
Strategy #22: Establish a Community Network

Arguably the most transformative group I have ever worked with was the community network that we launched at Camelback. With the help of my mentor, in partnership with a local philanthropy group, Social Venture Partners, we established a highly engaged, highly effective group of community leaders that helped lead critical initiatives aimed at improving climate and culture on campus. Still today, one decade and two principals later, the *Camelback Community Network* is just as engaged as it was then.

There are several reasons why this group has been so successful. The group was not formed to launch programs or initiatives (though it eventually did). The group was not formed to tell me how to improve teaching and learning (that wasn't the forte of the members). The group was also not formed to help individual companies or non-profits push their own agendas. Simply, the community network existed to support me, the staff, our vision, and our initiatives. The network gave me legal and personnel advice, helped me sharpen messaging and communication with staff and community, and, when appropriate, helped me create and launch new initiatives.

The key to a successful community network is selecting the right people and setting a clear purpose. Below is some practical advice on how and where to begin.

The People

It is critically important that you select a very diverse team – by diverse, I mean individuals with different personal **and** professional backgrounds. It wouldn't be helpful, for example, if the entire community network was made up of attorneys. One or two attorneys would be a huge asset – a room full not so much. Likewise, a community network of people only from the field of technology wouldn't yield the necessary results. In some ways, they would be extremely helpful to push the boundaries on technology in schools, but their scope or perspective would be too narrow.

With that being said, below is a list of some people and positions that would provide the best perspective and resources to a community network. This is not an exhaustive list, nor is it necessary to have all of these individuals on a community network – it's simply a starting point: human resource manager, attorney, entrepreneur, an individual from the technology field, a pastor or an employee of a local church, a restaurant owner, someone from the construction trade(s), someone in wealth management, former politician or legislator, and even a retired school or district leader.

If you would like to start your own network and are saying to yourself, "I don't know anyone like that" or "There are no people or businesses like that in my community," here is some advice. Much like the suggestion in a previous chapter about driving the neighborhood, there are surely businesses in your community. Granted, you may not be surrounded by major industries, but there are always small or chain businesses near your school. Someone owns that Circle K on the corner. There is a manager of the bank down the street. There is a franchise owner of the Subway or Panda Express a mile down the road. There are attorneys in every community – or, in the least, there are attorneys that do business in every community.

Start somewhere. Invite local business owners to a meeting, tell them your story and the story of your school, and invite them to engage in a monthly or quarterly meetings as a sounding board or an advisory committee for you. Tell them they'll never be asked directly to write a check or volunteer any more time than they want to or for which they have time. What you'll find is that there are plenty of people in business and industry who want to help make a difference in the lives of children and in education in general.

The final couple pieces of advice are this. Ultimately, you do want to build a team that is willing to give time, talent, and treasure. That may not be how you get it started, but eventually you want people on your community network who are willing to volunteer time and even donate funds – either personally or through their business. Much like a political campaign that is always looking for the three "W's" (workers, wisdom, wealth), school leaders should work to have a network of people who bring different skills, talents, and abilities.

Finally, the last piece of advice is this: don't put any vendors or local non-profits who stand to gain financially from engaging in this group. I have run into this on a couple of occasions. Having people with personal, professional, or financial agendas risks the impact and sustainability of this team. Be honest with the group up front – this is a team designed to selflessly make an impact in the day and lives of a school, and the staff and students it serves. Of course, that does not mean that a school shouldn't informally or formally partner with local community-based organizations, non-profits, or even vendors – schools should. But for the purposes of building a community network, make sure no-one stands to profit financially in any way.

The Projects

To give you an idea as to how powerful a highly engaged community network can be, below is a list some of the amazing work that this network did. As it turns out, some of the most game-changing and unique initiatives launched during my tenure originated from this community network – even though the team was not built to develop or implement programs. Here are a few examples:

Ritz Carlton Customer Service Training: The Community Network recognized that the school, in general, had terrible customer service. There were some individuals, of course, who had amazing customer service. However, there was no specific expectation or initiative that focused on exceptional customer service for students, staff, parents, or community. So, the community network hired the Ritz Carlton to train the entire staff on best practices in customer service. That led to the staff creating a customer service steering committee. That committee then developed, implemented, and monitored new customer service standards that radically changed the way Camelback approached customer service.

Office Furniture: As a part of the customer service initiative, the network decided that it was important that the front office looked and felt like a first-class business, not a stale doctor's office. So, the network made arrangements to acquire used (yet extremely nice) office furniture to change the look and feel of the front office. They also paid to have the entire office painted to match the new furniture.

Food and Clothing Bank: After learning about the poverty levels and struggles of students and parents, the network, in partnership with several local churches, launched a fully operational food and clothing bank that still exists today.

Gap Scholarship: When the community network became aware that students at Camelback would turn down $100,000 scholarship offers to private schools because of a $2,500-5,000 tuition gap, they sprung into action. They established the Camelback Gap Scholarship Fund and still raise over $50,000 per year for Camelback graduates. For more details, check out the Camelback Scholarship Fund at www.azfoundation.org.

Peer Tutoring: When Camelback established a requirement that every single student who was failing one or more classes had to attend mandatory tutoring, the community network flew a community member to Memphis to study a peer tutoring program there (called Peer Power ™). That community member, Diane, brought back her findings and helped the team implement a comprehensive peer tutoring program.

Coffee Shop: I decided that I wanted to open up a student-run coffee shop on campus. Students and staff could get cheaper and more convenient coffee at school. Students could also hand-deliver coffee to teachers during class as a service to them (how nice would that be as a teacher). I needed seed money to get it started, so the community network fronted the money to buy the materials.

Fashion Club: There was a budding yet struggling Fashion Club on campus. Members of the community network happened to be connected to a couple local retail stores. They connected the club sponsors with these local businesses, and, needless to say, the Fashion Club was taken to a whole different level.

Career Fair: When the network found out that Camelback didn't have a robust annual Career Fair, they helped our Student Government class organize a massive annual Career Fair.

Sand Volleyball Court: I always wanted our students to have a sand volleyball court on campus. If upper-middle class schools could have them, why not the inner city? With the help of the network, a generous donor came forward to underwrite the project and a sand volleyball court was built, speakers and bleachers installed, and free time at Camelback became that much more enjoyable.

Game Room: In one of the common areas, I decided to create an amazing game room for students to give them more to do before school, during lunch, and after school. I wanted pool tables, ping pong tables, air hockey tables, and other fun games. So, I asked the network to help me acquire items for the room. Before long, the room was full of games.

College Room: One of the biggest complaints from our counselors was that we didn't have computers that were dedicated solely to college admissions and college scholarship applications. So, I asked the network if they knew of a company in Phoenix that would be willing to sponsor a College Room, and they found one – Greenberg Traurig Law Firm. We set aside an entire classroom, next to the Game Room, for a beautiful College Room. They bought computers, printers, tables, chairs, couches, and college pennants from throughout the country.

Beautification: One of the community network members had a passion for gardening and landscaping. When I announced that I wanted to make a plan to launch a campus beautification project, the network stepped up. They had a local nursery donate trees, flowers, and even the labor. Today, the school has beautiful, mature trees that welcome all visitors to the front of the school.

Dinner Series: Since the Free and Reduced Lunch rate at Camelback was near 90%, most of the students had never had the opportunity to enjoy fine dining. My mentor offered to take six students out to dinner with six of his friends and colleagues to a local French restaurant. It turned out to be such an inspiring evening for both the students and the adults that we arranged for a second dinner – six new students, six new community members. That dinner turned out to be even more impacting than the first. Now, a decade later, the *Camelback Dinner Series* continues. Two other high schools in my district have begun dinner series and are experiencing the same level of success and inspiration.

Chapter 9
Review, Research, Reflect, Redesign
Allocate time and space for individuals and teams to reflect upon the current performance level(s) of the school as well as study successful schools, school models, and people to drive future vision, goals, and initiatives

In Chapter 7, I said that one of the first jobs of a leader is to fix the fixables, not create change. I said that short-term wins – solving problems and removing barriers – were critically important for new leaders. Short-term wins build goodwill, credibility, momentum – leaders need as much of these as possible before starting the actual change process.

Change can be very painful for individuals and entire school communities. Spencer Johnson in *Who Moved My Cheese* reminds us that people naturally prefer security and stability over change. Change often creates worry, frustration, and anxiety. Fear and frustration often lead to resistance. Resistance is detrimental to the change process.

This certainly does not mean that a leader should avoid change. Schools must constantly change, evolve, and improve to remain relevant and stay competitive, especially in today's choice-rich environment. I think Louise Penny said it best when she stated, "Life is change. If you aren't growing or evolving, you're standing still, and the rest of the world is surging ahead." That is more true in education today than ever before.

The ultimate goal of *Build Relationships, Enhancing Your Institutional Knowledge, Fix the Fixables,* and *Establish Leadership, Learning, and Listening Structures* is so that a leader can create the conditions for change. Highly effective leaders create change-ready people and places. This is a very intentional process. That is why we build relationships and fix problems first. That's why we establish leadership teams and learn as much about the school's culture, climate, and history as possible. That's why we worry about the needs of others first before we begin to ask others to meet our needs. Leaders and followers have different "wants and worries." Schools operate much like Maslow's Hierarchy of Needs. You can't get to the top of the pyramid without first addressing the bottom. You can't ask for teachers and staff to be risk-takers and change-makers if you haven't first met their basic needs and proven you can be trusted.

Reviewing, researching, and reflecting intentionally with a team or teams requires that structures and relationships have been established first. It's difficult to have honest and authentic conversations about school improvement and the change process if the foundation has not been laid. Ideally, for this component to be effective, a leader has launched and successfully established the two-team approach mentioned in the previous chapter. It is these two teams – an academic team and a non-academic team – that will help lead this component. But before embarking upon this phase, be sure that your campus and community – especially your leadership teams – have developed the relationships and respect necessary to start the change process.

The rest of this chapter is designed to give leaders a simple, practical, yet logical sequence for how to prepare for, design, and launch change. We'll start with identifying the problems and needs.

Review, Research, Reflect, Redesign Strategy #23: Know the Data

Much like the idea of becoming the chief historian, knowing your school's data is critically important. Every decision made on a campus – from changing a teacher's classroom to adjusting the lunch schedule to changing morning drop-off procedures – must be driven by intelligence or data. Unfortunately, leaders today typically make two major mistakes when it comes to data.

First, they go at it alone. Since most decisions should be made in concert with others, it's just as important for key stakeholders to know the data just as well as the leader. Nearly 30 years ago, Beer, Eisenstat, and Spectors wrote about the importance of "mobilizing commitment to change through joint diagnosis." Three decades later, this idea of "joint diagnosis" of key data points is just as relevant. Too often today, leaders study and evaluate data in isolation and, in doing so, miss a golden opportunity to build commitment and consensus through shared study and evaluation of key indicators.

Second, they focus only on literacy and numeracy. If leaders want to create lasting change, shift climate and culture, build sustainable systems, and drive student achievement in every way, they must look far beyond reading and math data. This is a trap into which so many school and even district leaders fall. Although literacy and numeracy drive school accountability today, there are many other indicators and data points leaders and their teams should know and analyze. Some of this data is easily accessible. Some may require time and resources to gather. Other data may need to be created from scratch. Nevertheless, here is a comprehensive list of data that your team should review.

> **Achievement:** Teams must look far beyond just state accountability measures.

>> **State Test Scores:** Every state has one (or multiple) state-adopted exams used to label schools. Although these exams don't typically offer data at a disaggregated enough level to inform teaching, teams should know all they can about the data and labeling system.

>> **District or School-Based Summative and Benchmark Data:** Often, districts and schools

have quarterly, semesterly, and/or annual exams. These are typically more informative than state exams, yet not often as helpful as Common Formative Assessment data.

Common Formative Assessments (CFAs): If your teachers or teacher teams, such as PLCs, aren't yet creating and using CFAs, this would be a great Year 2 or Year 3 initiative. CFAs can play a major role in improving teaching and learning outcomes because of the frequency and timeliness of the data.

Credit Currency: Credit currency is one of the best predictors of high school graduation, so this should be known and tracked closely. Are your freshmen largely on track to graduate? Are there subjects that seem to be barriers to credit currency (in other words, are there large percentages of students who are credit deficient in math)? What about juniors and seniors? Are there any master schedule adjustments that need to be made to improve currency?

A-F Rates: When I was principal at Camelback, I read an article about a sister district that analyzed the A-F rates of their freshmen and discovered that over one-third of their freshmen were failing. I remember thinking to myself, "Thank God we're not that bad." And then I realized I had never actually checked ours. So I had my registrar print me A-F rates of our 9th graders and, much to my dismay, over 50% of our freshmen were failing at least one course. It was that discovery that led to our school-wide peer tutoring program, Success Is Mandatory.

For the remainder of my tenure, I tracked A-B and D-F rates closely. Truthfully, teachers hate it when you track their grading practices, so be careful. However, because there is so much on the line for students, this is one area that I wasn't afraid to discuss with teachers even if it harmed relations.

I remember one particular teacher who had a long history (well before my time) of failing the majority of his students. Year after year, his failure rates would reach as high as 90%. Yes, 90%. I met with him often about his grades to put plans in place to reduce failure rates. Nothing was working, so I had to get more forceful to save students from being harmed. I scheduled a meeting with him to discuss me taking away his honors courses and, instead, giving him an alternative assignment. He walked in the room, took out his recorder, laid it in the middle of the table, and said, "So, what is it you'd like to talk about?"

I leaned in toward the middle of the table, put my mouth just a few inches from the recorder, and responded, "The fact that you continue to fail 90% of your honors students, and I'm now convinced you are the problem."

Post-Institution Success: Not only should teams study trends in drop-out and graduation rates (in high schools), schools should also do their best to acquire data on what I call "post-institution success." Elementary schools should know how successful (or not) their students are when they transition to middle school; likewise, middle schools should know how successful their students are when they move on to high school. Are they passing their classes? Are they taking honors or AP courses? Are they dropping out early or graduating at high rates? High schools should also track post-institution success very closely. Are students going to community colleges? Are they going straight to universities? What about trade schools? In my current district, we allocate funds to upload all of our graduates into the NCAA Clearinghouse so that we can track not only college matriculation rates but also college completion rates.

Evaluations: Teacher and staff evaluations are also important data points to track. Of course, this must be done first by the principal and identities should always be protected. Any relevant data – trends, concerns, celebrations – can be shared with the leadership teams.

Discipline: Understanding a school's discipline data is critically important. Student behavior – a topic in the next chapter – has a direct impact on school culture and climate. I always start with looking at the basics – who, what, when, where, and why. Here are types of questions I ask:

> **Who:** Are there teachers who write all of the referrals? You want to know this, not because you want to punish those teachers, but so that you can provide better support and professional development.   Is there a small percentage of students who are getting the majority of the referrals (or taking up the majority of administration's time)?

> **What:** What are the most common infractions? Are they violent or just disruptive? Are they major classroom disruptions or minor issues like talking or pencil stealing? Does your school

have a drug problem? What about racism? Or disrespect to staff?

When: Are referrals happening before or after school? During passing periods? At lunch? During instructional time? When I was an elementary school assistant principal, I found out that almost half of all school-wide referrals happened at lunch time, on the playground, and involved issues with soda and Hot Cheetos (true story). I banned soda and Hot Cheetos and literally cut the time I spent on discipline in half.

Where: Do most of the problems happen on the playground? In the hallways? In the bathrooms? In the park down the road? At the corner store? In classrooms? In the gymnasium?

Why: Though this may be difficult to determine on the surface, are there reasons why discipline is happening? Do you not have enough playground aides? Are lunch lines too long, which cause fights in line? Are there bathroom areas on campus that are largely unsupervised?

Attendance: Teams should also have a good grasp of attendance issues. Are students tardy often? Do upper grades have worse attendance than lower grades? Are school-wide attendance rates trending in the right or wrong direction?

Retention: Retention is vitally important to a school's success. Some turnover is healthy – but you want to make sure that, year after year, your best staff is staying. Your teams should know what the overall staff turnover rate is on campus. And then the team should break that data down to the employee group level. Do custodians turnover frequently? How is your teacher retention? Do most first-year teachers quit after one year? After two? What about student retention – does your enrollment increase or decrease throughout the year? Are there times of year that students tend to leave?

Crime and Community: It is also wise to know as much about community data as possible. Are parks dangerous? Are there problem areas in the neighborhood? Does your zip code have major issues with drugs, violence, trafficking, prostitution? Perhaps your school is in a safer neighborhood, so you may want to know how many of your students play little league or use the Boys & Girls Club. Are there churches in your area that could be a huge resource to your school?

General Student Information: How many languages do your students speak? What percentage of your students are being raised by a single parent or grandparent? Are there areas of your community that are extremely impoverished?

Budget: Your teams should also know how you spend your money. How much money do you spend on paper and dry erase markers? What about soap and toilet paper? You may be able to find some savings in these areas that can be re-allocated to the classroom. Do you spend enough money on professional development? What about tutoring? Do you have a budget for playground or sports equipment? Are you spending more on boys sports than you are girls?

Staff Opinion: Finally, I think staff opinions, attitudes, and beliefs matter. Your teams should know what their colleagues think. This is often best done in school-wide culture and climate surveys. There are many great examples of these online. Forums and focus groups are also great ways to dig deeper. They often yield the same or similar results as a survey but enable teams to ask questions and get below the surface – peel back the layers of the onion, so to speak.

After we launched the Organizational Cabinet at Camelback, we began listening sessions in the library. Anyone from the staff could show up to share their thoughts, concerns, celebrations, frustrations. For literally a month – four consecutive Tuesdays after school for over an hour each time – I stood by an easel pad making notes of everything that was good, bad, and ugly about Camelback. I heard about everything from terrible administration to an award-winning marketing program to students who didn't bring backpacks to school to the bathrooms on the south of campus that had become terribly problematic. I have since named these "dump your crap" or DYC sessions. These DYC sessions became such an important part of the healing process for Camelback. It was the first time in over two decades that staff was able to share their thoughts and opinions – both positive and negative – in a safe, public setting.

After four weeks of listening, we had pages and pages of notes. We then spent another month organizing the feedback. We looked for trends and commonalities. We determined which issues were academic and which were non-academic. We discussed which were school issues and which could be considered community issues. We made lists of staff issues and lists of student issues. We determined which issues we could control and which we could not. By the end of the few weeks, after hours of dialogue, we narrowed all of the feedback down to less than ten major themes or trends (such as students don't feel connected to school and students aren't taking advantage of out-of-school-time opportunities). Throughout this phase, I didn't allow the teams to begin "solutioning." Granted, there were plenty of opinions about how to solve these problems, but this wasn't the time. This was simply phase one in an intentional process.

Once we had all the data we needed, and had it categorized, we set it all aside until we were ready for it later in the process. We had much more learning to do together before we began to generate solutions.

Review, Research, Reflect, Redesign Strategy #24: Know What the Research Says

In the medical field, there is a large body of research and theory on what scholars call *informed decision-making*. The idea behind *informed decision-making* is that doctors and teams make medical decisions based on facts, information, data, and statistics – not on past experiences, opinions, beliefs, and even "gut reactions." In the medical field where decisions often have life or death implications, medical professionals are trained to analyze information and facts to determine treatment plans, prescription dosages, anesthetics, and even release dates from a medical facility.

Although decision-making in education is not life or death (although emergency planning during these difficult times in our country can be), there are definitely lives and futures at stake every day in schools. As educational attainment is still one of the strongest predictors of future success and financial stability, schools must be driven by the same commitment to quality decision-making as the medical profession. In many ways, this entire chapter is an ode to *informed decision-making*.

It is critically important for teams to be well-studied, versed, and steeped in research and theory. Education, much like medicine and finance, has an expansive body of research. Schools and leadership teams cannot ignore research and make major school improvement decisions based solely on beliefs and experiences that sell their students and colleagues short. Often our own personal experiences are terribly limited. That is not to say that staff experience and expertise do not play a major role in the change process – they do. However, building a much stronger knowledge base of school leaders and teams is enormously important if the ultimate goal is radically different results for students and staff.

After our Organizational Cabinet had completed the DYC sessions, had categorized the feedback, and set the findings aside, we began to read research together. I remember the first book we ever read together: *Breaking Ranks II: Strategies for Leading High School Reform*. This book, published by the National Association of Secondary School Principals, or NASSP, wet the appetite of our team to become not only leaders in the area of school reform, but learners as well. This book propelled us into a season of study that was transformative – it pushed us far beyond our own experiences and into research-based strategies and structures that we would otherwise have not discovered and, ultimately, implemented. Instead of listing pages of specific research articles and resources, I have compiled a list of research topics that your team should consider depending on your areas of focus or need.

> **Elementary, Middle, and High School Reform:** Much like *Breaking Ranks*, there are several books and research articles on K-12 school reform. Your teams should immerse themselves in the basic research surrounding school improvement.

> **Teaching and Pedagogy:** Many struggling schools today have struggling teachers who rely upon antiquated teaching strategies. There are plenty of books and research articles on teaching strategies that yield results – find a few like *Teach Like a Champion* and

challenge your teams to think differently about their craft.

Student Learning and the Brain: If your teams (and your school in general) do not have a basic understanding of the brain, books like *Brain Rules* can serve as a catalyst to get your staff to examine and question curriculum and pedagogy in the context of student learning.

Adult Learning and Professional Development: Likewise, it is tremendously important that your key leaders are well-versed in adult learning and its implications on professional development.

Assessment: Shifts or changes made to teaching, learning, and professional development should be informed by data. We get the vast majority of our data in schools through assessments. Therefore, your team should thoroughly understand the differences between summative, formative, criterion, mastery-based, and other forms of assessments and how they can be used to improve outcomes. *Assessment for Learning* may be a good place to start.

Intervention and Enrichment: In schools that subscribe to the traditional PLC model, there are four questions that every team must consider: what is it that we want kids to learn and be able to do; how will we know if they learned it; what will we do if they don't; what will we do if they do. The last two questions allude to interventions and enrichment opportunities. Few students in any given class will progress at the perfect pace and master new concepts just as the teacher designed. Instead, many students will require interventions to stay on track while others will master concepts quickly and need other opportunities to enrich their learning to stay challenged and engaged. Your teams should know the research surrounding enrichment and intervention, such as *Response to Intervention* (RTI), to better support teachers in lesson and assessment design.

Bell and Master Schedules: For middle school and high school teams, studying the research behind effective bell schedules and master schedules is critical. Are classes too long? Are there enough breaks built into the school day? Should your campus consider block scheduling? How do you ensure that students who require extra remedial courses also have access to electives? Is there enough rigor (honors and AP courses) built into the schedule?

Advisory, House, and Cohort Systems: In larger middle and high schools, making sure that every student is known and held accountable is essential. Often, the only way to guarantee this level of personalization is through advisory, house, or cohort systems. Your team should research these models to see if any would work within your school's current structure – or, if they don't, perhaps it's time to consider a completely different structure or model. Your team should also know the research behind personalized learning.

Connectedness: Of all of the research on the market about students and schools, I believe this is one of the most important areas. The Centers for Disease Control and Prevention describes *connectedness* as the belief held by students that the adults and peers in their school care about their learning as well as about them as individuals (we will discuss this in-depth in Chapter

10). I can't imagine anything more important and impacting to a student than being and feeling connected.

College Counseling: Finally, and this is obviously just for high schools, does your team (or, in the least, your counseling department) know the research behind effective college counseling? Does your school have the right programs and pathways that lead to college? Do you offer the right type of financial aid and scholarship support? Are there a couple best practices in college counseling that could have a dramatic impact on college matriculation rates for your seniors?

Although this may not be an exhaustive list, it is a great start for any team or teams looking to make more informed decisions about school reform. In fact, this may very well be too much. Pace yourself and your teams. You can't read it all. If you know that your school needs to personalize learning and make students feel more connected, you may want to narrow your research on master scheduling, cohort systems, and connectedness. If your school already has school-wide instructional strategies, you may want to narrow your focus on brain research, assessment, and enrichment. As I've said before, since every school community is unique, only you will know what is most appropriate for your school.

In order to empower her leadership teams and inform the work they were embarking upon, Megan incorporated the study of research on effective schools into her teams' work. In her first year, both her Mission Cabinet and Vision Cabinet studied Lawrence Lezotte's *Correlates of Effective Schools* as well as the *Nine Characteristics of High-Performing Schools* from the Office of the Washington State Superintendent of Public Instruction. Both resources were short, but comprehensive, with many similarities.

During the Cabinets' monthly meetings, they spent roughly half their time engaged in focused conversations on the research. They worked one characteristic or correlate at a time, with independent reading and reflection and then a group discussion. As they read, they took notes on the following:

Ideas I already knew
Ideas I didn't know
What we are currently doing (aligned with this characteristic/correlate)
What we are not doing (aligned with this characteristic/correlate)
Concrete takeaways

The entire process took approximately three months and resulted in all Cabinet members having a clear understanding of what the school needed to prioritize. From there, they were able to set goals for what they wanted to accomplish during the current school year, such as developing a vision for the school, and beyond.

During Megan's second year, the Cabinets extended their research by engaging in a book study of Lezotte's *What Effective Schools Do Differently: Re-Envisioning the Correlates.* This text gave much more detail into the correlates and also provided substantial practical applications and approaches to consider. Prior to beginning the book study, the cabinets identified which chapters/correlates aligned to the work of Mission Cabinet, which aligned to the work of Vision Cabinet, and which aligned to both. They then mapped out which chapters to which each Cabinet would read and respond. As a result of this work, the teams prioritized developing a clear mission statement for the school and creating collaborative structures in sync with Professional Learning Communities.

Reading, studying, analyzing research and best practices is a powerful experience for both individuals and teams. Teams build stronger bonds and relationships. Conversations and discussions are elevated far beyond experience and emotion. Decisions and compromises become more strategic and intentional. Ultimately, the goal of better decisions is better outcomes.

<u>R</u>eview, Research, Reflect, Redesign Strategy #25: Know What Exemplary Schools Are Doing (and Go Visit Them)

One of the only drawbacks of scholarly research is that it can often feel theoretical and can be difficult to connect to current practice. It's extremely important that as you choose research for your team you choose research that is practical. If you allow your team to find and recommend research, make sure they find research that is aligned and useful to your work. Likewise, if you lead book studies, find books that connect easily to your current reality as a school community.

One way to take research and study to the next level is to also study successful schools and school models. Instead of just reading about the research behind PLCs, read a case study about a school that has exemplary PLCs. If you want to learn more about successful advisory programs, read the research **and** observe a school in your area that has an effective advisory system. Likewise, if your most pressing issue is improving student behavior, you should read theories and research on behavior modification first, and then go visit schools that have implemented school-wide discipline programs.

In my school district today, we have two major initiatives on the horizon. The first is to completely re-think large, traditional, comprehensive campus models. The second is to implement restorative justice/restorative practices district-wide. Instead of simply reading books and research on the topics, which we have done, we are sending teams to observe model programs. Over the past couple of years, we have flown teams to Denver and Chicago to observe restorative practices in action. We have flown teams to Nashville to study how they transformed their comprehensive campuses into smaller learning academies. Our teams would argue that, although understanding the research behind these innovations is necessary, the firsthand visits have been most transformative.

When I was at Camelback, among the many issues that we identified, our Advanced Placement, or AP, scores were dismal. Candidly, they were embarrassing. The average AP score school-wide was less than two. Considering AP scores are based on a 1-5 scale, 1 being the lowest, our AP program was in serious trouble. Instead of flying our teachers to AP conferences in some other part of the country, I called the College Board to ask them if they could identify 2-3 schools in the state of Arizona that had the best AP scores. They gave me two that were within driving distance. Not surprisingly, both were in very upper-middle class neighborhoods in the valley. Nevertheless, there had to be something we could learn from these schools. So, one day, I traveled to one of the schools, Pinnacle High School, and spent a half day with the principal learning all about their AP program – how they selected students, how they built it into the master schedule, how they selected and trained teachers.

Later that same month, I took all of our AP teachers to observe another school – one of the most upper class private schools in Arizona. Many of our teachers were highly skeptical. I heard comments like, "What can we learn from them? I mean, if I had a classroom full of privileged gifted students I'd have good AP scores, too." Another staff member said, "I'm only going to see if I can steal some of their curriculum. I'm definitely not going to learn anything from this visit, but I can at least get some materials." I knew that if they could observe with an open mind, it could be an amazing learning experience. And it was.

We saw so many different strategies, structures, and systems, far beyond AP, that informed our work as a team in the coming years. Sure, they served a completely different student population. Our kids were poor and minority. Their kids were rich and white. They had parent engagement of which low-income schools could only dream. But we left that day with so many new ideas and realizations. One of the biggest realizations was that in every class we observed, the students were doing all the work – they taught classes, led discussions, and developed projects. At Camelback, our teachers did all the work – they lectured most of the period, were the center of all large- and small-group discussions, and were intimately involved in all projects and presentations. No wonder why their students aced the exam – they were forced to know, lead, and teach the material. Our students had to take notes, study for quizzes, and complete hours of homework memorizing concepts.

Another great takeaway that day was their unique bell schedule. At the time, we were convinced that longer class periods meant more learning. We were considering reducing class periods from 55 to 52 minutes at the time to create the new advisory period. The vast majority of the teachers on campus hated the idea, especially arts, athletics, and science teachers. But when we asked to see their bell schedule, we saw that they had 44 minute classes. Shorter class periods allowed for more periods in a day, more study halls, more electives, and more intervention classes. It also allowed them to create a 20-minute mid-morning break that they called, "Community Time." In many ways, it was a brain break and community-building time. Teachers loved it because they got a healthy 20-minute break in the middle of the morning. Students loved it for a number of reasons. And the booster clubs and parent groups loved it because they sold snacks and school gear during that time. Although we never officially implemented a mid-morning break, we did decide to reduce our class periods from 55 to 50 to allow for more minutes during our advisory period.

Review, Research, Reflect, Redesign Strategy #26: Interview Great People

A few years ago, I led a search committee to find a new pastor at a small Lutheran church in Phoenix. The committee went through a very similar process that we've discussed in this chapter. First, the committee analyzed the data – finances, membership, outreach, etc. The team then gathered input from church members on what they were looking for in the next pastor. Then the committee looked at other Lutheran churches in the area and across the country that were growing and thriving. Candidly, it was difficult to find many great examples. If you know anything about denominational churches today, many are experiencing a steady decline in membership and giving. It is the bible-based, non-denominational churches that are growing and thriving.

The search committee then decided to meet with a local pastor of a booming bible-based church. Much like Camelback visiting the private school, these two institutions had little in common. However, interviewing this pastor to ask about his approach to leadership, his approach to church finance, and his approach to preaching and ministry gave the search committee a whole new perspective on pastoral leadership. This new perspective guided the rest of the search process.

Throughout my career – as an assistant principal, principal, director, and now superintendent – I could make a strong argument that I have grown more from interviewing and meeting exemplary leaders than I have reading about or visiting exemplary organizations. As I was preparing to become a high school principal, I scheduled as many breakfast, lunch, and coffee meetings as I could with exemplary high school principals. When I became a superintendent, I made a list of 5-10 successful current or retired superintendents in Arizona, handed it to my secretary, and made time to meet with as many of them as possible.

I do not limit myself to only educational leaders. Much like the purpose of the *Community Network* mentioned in Chapter 8, educators and educational leaders can benefit greatly from the time, talent, and treasures of those outside of the field of education. The same goes for your leadership teams – interviewing great leaders and entrepreneurs outside of education can really expand the thinking and perspective of the individuals on your team.

In any given community, city, or region, there are amazingly talented and innovative people who would be willing to give up an hour of their time to help you and your team. In any region of this country, especially in larger cities, there will be Chambers of Commerce, Rotary clubs, and CEO groups (in Phoenix, for example, we have Greater Phoenix Leadership) that would love to connect your school with local leaders. There are also large utility companies and other major industries in your area regardless of your zip code. Call their President's or CEO's office, introduce yourself, and explain what you are looking for – you'll never be told no.

Preparing for these interviews is even easier. I have teams generate a list of 10-15 questions that could be asked of any community leader. Then, depending on the type of leader that is coming to be interviewed, we tailor the questions to their industry. In other words, if you are interviewing a CEO of a local technology company, you'll want to focus most of your time on innovations in technology and systems that can impact schools. Likewise, if you are interviewing a partner of a local law firm, you may want to focus your questions more on personnel and legal issues. Either way, you want your questions to help inform your work as school leaders.

Finally, keep these three thoughts in mind as you consider interviews of community leaders. First, make sure you have simple refreshments for your guest. Purchase water, soda, and even light snacks. Even if she or he doesn't take any, you want be as hospitable as possible. This leads to the second thought. Interviewing community leaders is, in many ways, a branding and marketing exercise. You want that leader to leave your school talking about how impressed she or he is. You want that leader to go back into the community and say wonderful things about your school. Finally, you are building a network for your school. In the non-profit world, they call this "friendraising." Use these interviews as vehicles to grow a network of supporters that you can call on for Career Fairs, your budding Community Network, or your end-of-the-year Teacher Appreciation luncheon.

<u>R</u>eview, Research, Reflect, Redesign Strategy #27: Reflect, Connect, Launch

By this point, your teams should be well-equipped to begin problem-solving and *solutioning*. They should know and be able to articulate much of the important data about your school. They should know the issues – the attitudes, beliefs, opinions of the staff. They should be well-versed in research and best practices in education today. They should be able to tell stories about exemplary schools and what they liked and didn't like. And, finally, they should have ideas and innovations in mind that they have learned from community leaders.

Next, you and your team should engage in a simple yet comprehensive four-step process to bring all of this together.

1) **Analyze the Learning:** Your team(s) should spend time analyzing all of the research, best practices, model schools, and exemplary leaders. The goal of this step is to generate major themes and takeaways. Are there pieces of research or even best practices that seem to be a perfect fit for your school? Are there programs or initiatives that you learned from exemplary schools or community leaders that can be replicated? Was there a case study you read that

seemed to mirror the reform efforts you envision for your school? By the end of this phase, your team should come away with a list of 10-15 major takeaways, findings, or potential programs or initiatives.

2) **Revisit Your Data:** Next, your teams should bring all of the school and community data you analyzed earlier in this process, including your DYC data. As a team, revisit those major themes and findings that you generated earlier. Now that you've had a chance to learn and grow together, these conversations should look, feel, and sound very differently. Before teams are properly equipped to lead school reform, much of the conversation is typically negative and narrowly focused on small problems on campus. After teams have studied and researched best practices and models, the dialogue shifts to ideas, innovations, and initiatives that can transform school culture and student outcomes.

3) **Make Connections:** At this point, your teams should have a list of 10-15 major takeaways or themes learned from the research phase as well as 10-15 major trends or themes from the data analysis and DYC sessions. Now it is time for your teams to begin to connect their learning with campus issues. Are there campus issues that can be solved using research or best practices? Are there systems or structures that you observed at exemplary schools that can be implemented on your campus that could resolve some of the major concerns brought up by your staff. In short, *Making Connections* is simply

cross-walking your findings/learnings with your campus issues/trends.

4) **Identify and Implement Innovations:** Finally, your teams should begin to develop initiatives and innovations that will drive change. These innovations (programs, structures, systems) should, as best as possible, be research-based and proven practices that have the potential to not only improve achievement yet also solve some of the issues that surfaced through data analysis and staff feedback sessions (i.e. DYC sessions). Ideally, one new innovation can solve multiple problems at the same time.

One of the best examples of this at Camelback was the advisory program. When we analyzed our data and themed the feedback from our staff, there were three major issues that our team identified: students lacked connections to adults, students didn't take advantage of opportunities offered such as tutoring or clubs; students lacked study skills and didn't complete homework consistently. When we researched personalization and connectedness, our studies led us to an in-depth look at advisory programs, house systems, and cohort models. Eventually, our team determined that a robust advisory program would solve all three of the aforementioned issues.

Although our advisory program is much too complex to describe in one paragraph, here are some highlights to show you how it addressed multiple problems at the same time. Each student was assigned to an "advisor," which was a teacher on campus. Since *looping* – staying with the same teacher for two or more years – is still one of the most effective practices in education, students were assigned to the same advisor all four years. Students in each advisory (about 20-25 students) had the same counselor and were also assigned to the same administrator – either the principal or an assistant principal. Four days per week in advisory, students traveled to tutoring centers or to teachers' classrooms to get help, make up missed work, or re-take exams. Students who didn't travel could use advisory as a study hall. Students who were failing one or more classes were required to travel to get tutoring. One day per week was an actual *advisory* day – advisors would check grades and attendance. They'd also engage in team- and community-building activities as an advisory class. The final major component of advisory was a mandatory engagement requirement – all students had to complete community service hours, join a club or a sport, and attend 10 campus events per year (from an Open House to a girls volleyball game). These were tracked during advisory and were a part of the *Spartan SHIELD* that you'll read about later. As you can see, one innovation – advisory – addressed multiple issues identified through the research process.

Another issue identified was that our teachers lacked connections to each other. Part of the issue was that, over the years, departments became physically separated. Math teachers had classrooms in the 2000, 3000, and the 4000 building. Algebra teachers literally had to walk 5 minutes to speak with a fellow algebra teacher. Departments also complained that they couldn't get together frequently enough – both formally and informally – because they never saw each other. Our research on PLCs made it painfully obvious that we needed to make major changes to classroom assignments. Granted, this isn't a fun process. Teachers hate to move classrooms. Have you ever tried to move 5 or even 10 teachers' classrooms? Well, believe it or not, over the summer between my first and second year at Camelback, we moved over 50 teachers' classrooms. It took a ton of planning and communication, but it yielded great results. We were not only able to get all math teachers in the same area, for example, we were able to create an algebra hallway, a geometry hallway, and an upper-level math hallway. Teacher connections became stronger, planning improved, and teams began to behave and function like true learning communities.

Although I will not go into detail in this book about implementation theory, I do want to share six brief thoughts for you and your teams to consider as you implement major changes. Just know that there are many books and research articles available on this topic if you feel as though you need more assistance with implementation.

> **Clear, Consistent Communication:** Although this seems to be the simplest part of the implementation process, it often turns out to be the biggest challenge. Change is difficult for most people, and without clear, consistent communication, change is downright painful. During times of major change, be sure to publish daily reminders, weekly messages, or monthly newsletters. If you have a television studio, film messages just for your staff. The more you communicate during the change process, the smoother the transition and the happier the people.

> **Head, Heart, Barriers:** In *Switch*, by Heath and Heath, we are reminded that in order for people to accept and support change, a leader must consider three things. First, for the logical thinkers on the staff, leaders must focus on the head. They must make rational, commonsense arguments for why the change is necessary. If logical thinkers don't see the rationale behind the change, they won't get on board. Second, for the people driven by emotions and feelings, the leaders must focus on the heart. They must appeal to the emotional side of people, convincing staff that this change will have a positive impact on the lives of staff,

students, and community. Finally, for all employees, a leader must remove any unnecessary barriers. Are there rules, regulations, procedures that may get in the way? Are there resources that teachers need to be successful? If you want to implement a school-wide mentoring program, for example, have your staff been trained on mentoring strategies?

Bullets, Then Cannonballs: This comes from Jim Collins' *Great by Choice*. Collins says that leaders should begin with low-risk, low-cost, low-effort changes to test ideas and theories (bullets). It is only after ideas and innovations have been tested and proven to be effective that a leader should implement high-risk, high-effort changes (cannonballs). As a leader, as you consider major changes, consider taking small steps to test new ideas before jumping in head first.

Fail Forward: John Maxwell, in *Failing Forward*, reminds leaders that they should see mistakes as stepping stones to success, view failure as temporary, and bounce back from challenges. Don't become discouraged by failure and challenges; instead, use them as motivation and learning lessons to improve your practices and programs.

Monitor and Adjust: Often, leaders and teams get so excited about, and have such ownership over, a new program or initiative that they become rigid and inflexible when it comes to making adjustments. No implementation is perfect, no program is perfect. Monitor progress consistently. Be open to making changes or shifting focus. You should even be willing to abandon an innovation that doesn't yield the results you need.

Success Breeds Success: Finally, don't ever forget this age old saying. There is great power behind success – it builds credibility and momentum. So, as you consider a handful of new changes, start with the ones that are most likely to succeed with the least amount of effort and time. Once people taste success, they'll be ready for the next challenge.

<u>R</u>eview, Research, Reflect, Redesign Strategy #28: If Needed, Rewrite Your Mission and Vision

Rewriting a vision or mission statement, much like changing a logo, is often a challenging process. Over time, people and communities become very connected to mission and vision statements, even when they are no longer relevant or inspirational. Even embarking upon a process to re-visit these can be controversial. However, despite the controversy, it may be time for a change if any one of the following applies: it's outdated and doesn't parallel the current realities of the school; it's long and doesn't resonate with the staff and community; it's uninspiring and doesn't align with the hopes, dreams, and aspirations of the staff.

In 2016, Glenn Smith published an article titled, *Seven Reasons Your Company Needs a Clear, Written Mission Statement.* Although the article was written for the business sector, it is just as germane to schools as it is any other sector. Here are the seven reasons:

1) It determines your direction
2) It focuses your future
3) It provides a template for decision-making
4) It keeps you aligned
5) It welcomes change
6) It shapes strategy
7) It facilitates evaluation and improvement

If anything, a clearly written and articulated mission and vision can serve as a "North Star" for you and your staff. Just be certain that your new mission statement is precise, meaningful, inspirational, and aspirational.

Inc.com recently released an article titled, *The 9 Worst Mission Statements of All Time*. It highlights some of the major mistakes companies make. Although I won't list them all here, here are a few highlights:

> **Too Wordy:** Avon's mission statement was 249 words and talked about everything from "increasing shareholder value to fighting breast cancer."

> **Too General:** Some mission statements are so general that you don't even know what the company does. Albertson's mission statement talked about the importance of their customers' "shopping experience" yet never mention that they are a grocery store.

> **Too Lofty:** Other companies draft mission statements that are so lofty they are impossible to attain. The article highlights a stick-on label company that claimed they will "make the world more intelligent" through their product.

> **Too Conceited:** The article also talked about MGM's mission statement that was so boastful that it could turn customers away. They remind leaders to "say what you aspire to be, not why you already think you're great."

The article had other lessons to be learned, including ensuring your statement has no spelling or grammatical areas. Sadly, that's often the case. The article also spoke about Dell who, at the time, had no mission statement. It argues, and I wholeheartedly agree, that the only thing worse than a bad mission statement is no mission at all.

From an educational perspective, I strongly encourage school leaders to craft short mission and vision statements that are goal-oriented. Long-winded, multiple sentence mission statements don't move organizations. School mission statements should clearly define the future and also serve as a call to action for staff, students, and community. Often when I use the phrase "goal-oriented," leaders ask me if they should talk about specific metrics in their statements, or even specifically write mission statements about their state's high stakes exam. As an example, I once read a mission statement in Arizona that said, "Jackson School will ensure that at least 80% of its students will meet state expectations on AIMS." AIMS was the state's exam at the time. There are obviously many issues with this statement, starting with the 20% of the students this particular school is satisfied leaving behind.

Below are the main mission/vision statements of Carl T. Smith and Norma Jones. What you'll see right away is that they are virtually the same, and that's obviously intentional. Both statements were based on the belief that schools that serve middle school students have two major responsibilities: ensure that students will be ready to succeed in high school **and** put students on a path to college. Most K-8 elementary schools and middle schools believe that their primary responsibility is to have strong student achievement during their years in elementary and middle school. That's only partially true. Instilling in students a belief that college is possible, and matching that with the skills and knowledge necessary to excel in high school, is the ultimate goal of primary education.

> **Carl T. Smith Middle School:** A Community of High School-Ready and College-Bound Readers, Leaders, and Achievers.

Norma Jones Vision Statement: A Community of High School-Ready and College- and Career-Bound Learners, Leaders, and Achievers.

Both of these statements are designed to be goal-oriented and highly actionable. In addition, every word has meaning. The use of *Community* in each statement is highly intentional – entire communities must own mission and vision statements. Listing the characteristics of a successful student (*Learners, Leaders, Achievers*, for example) is also very deliberate. Having such clarity in a statement compels a school to stay focused on key indicators. Finally, as mentioned above, the statement also ensures that the two schools stay focused on developing students who are high school-ready and college-bound.

Camelback's mission statement has a similar feel. It's built on a similar belief – that schools must prepare students for success at the next level, not just at the current level of schooling. It also lists specific qualities that a student should embody if they are to live up to the mission of the school.

CBHS Mission Statement: A Unified Community Dedicated to Building Students Worthy of the Spartan S.H.I.E.L.D. (Stewardship, Honor, Intelligence, Ethics, Leadership, Discipline)

At Camelback, becoming worthy of the Spartan SHIELD was the ultimate accomplishment. As a school, we determined how students could demonstrate that they were *worthy*. Students earned each of the six letters of the SHIELD by completing various tasks or maintaining certain levels of achievement. For example, in order to earn the "S" (Stewardship), students had to complete a specific number of community service hours. To earn the "I" (Intelligence), students had to pass all classes or, if they had failing grades, had to attend a specific number of tutoring hours. To make sure that the SHIELD was embedded into the fabric of the school, the components of the SHIELD were tracked during advisory, and that becoming *Worthy of the Spartan SHIELD* was the only way to receive credit for advisory.

As mentioned earlier, it is not necessary for a new leader to create a new mission statement, so do not change your statement unless your broader community agrees it is time for a change. As a prime example, my predecessor, through a lengthy process of engaging stakeholders, developed a clear and concise mission statement almost ten years ago. I have been in my current role now for three years and, until recently launching a re-branding process, I haven't even considered altering or rewriting the mission statement. Still, pending stakeholder feedback over the coming months, we may likely leave the mission untouched. Part of the reason this mission statement – *Preparing Every Student for Success in College, Career, and Life* – has had such staying power is because it's simple and focused on student outcomes.

The next chapter, ***Engage, Excite, and Establish Expectations for Students***, is all about student outcomes. Although the vast majority of this book has focused on adults (staff, parents, community partners) and adult behaviors, the main goal of all of the aforementioned efforts, from relationship building to creating leadership structures to redesigning campus initiatives, is to create enhanced learning conditions and higher achievement levels for students.

Chapter 10
Engage, Excite, and Establish Expectations for Students
Focus on improving pride, engagement, behaviors, and beliefs among students to expedite the improvement process

To start this chapter, I want to share two phrases that I use virtually every time I speak in front of students today. These two phrases are the basis for the twelve strategies that we'll cover in this chapter. They are at the core of *what* I do and *why* I do it. I would guess that after some reflection, you would agree that they are at the core of the *what* and *why* of your leadership journey as well.

"You are the reason we come to work every day."

As much as I love adults, and as much as I am committed to this idea of education, I do this work for kids. I put up with personnel issues and power struggles for kids. I navigate politics and policy so that leaders in my system can focus on kids. I trudge through meetings, events, and planning sessions with adults because I believe they will enhance the lives of kids. Everything I do, and the reason why I get up early in the morning still on fire for this vocation, is because I feel called to help change, shape, and better the lives of kids.

"We have two jobs: to love you and to hold you accountable."

I also believe strongly that we have responsibility to genuinely love kids and, at the same time, hold them accountable for reaching their full potential. This is not an *either or* proposition. We must do both. Too many educators today lean too heavily on the side of love. They coddle students. They set lower expectations, especially for students of color and students from low-income neighborhoods. They accept excuses and allow students to perform well below their potential. There are also too many educators who lean too heavily on the side of accountability. They show no love, empathy, and respect for students. They create classrooms and schools that resemble prisons and military bases. They don't believe in second chances or view mistakes as learning experiences. Zero tolerance rules the day.

I begin this chapter this way to make three very clear points.

First, although we spent the first 150 or so pages of this book focused almost entirely on adults in the system, we are in the business of kids. We must love our adults, know and care about them authentically, focus on their working environment, remove barriers and frustrations, and be fully committed to them as persons and professionals. Yet, while we focus on adults, let us never forget that we signed a contract to change the lives of young men and young women sitting in classrooms, playing on playgrounds, and competing in gymnasiums.

Second, we must love and believe in *all* kids. We must believe that every single student – the honor roll student you hand a certificate to at every assembly, the quiet kid you have never met, and the frequent flier that you know intimately because he is trying to break a referral record – has the potential and ability to thrive and excel with the right amount of love, support, and guidance. If you don't believe that all students can be successful, and I mean *all*, then you should question yourself and your commitment to this work. As Rick Miller with *Kids at Hope* says, *All Children Can Succeed, No Exceptions.*

Third, we must be willing to subscribe to the *tough love* model of parenting. Kids undoubtedly need love. But they also need boundaries and high expectations. They need structures and systems to hold them accountable to reaching their full potential. They need adults in their lives that push them. They need teachers who challenge them. They need coaches who don't give up on them even when they give up on themselves. I recently led a focus group of ten high school students with the intent of better understanding their general needs, academically, socially, emotionally. One student so eloquently responded, "You want to show me some respect? Challenge me. Don't accept my excuses. Don't hand me worksheets and sit at your desk. You want to show me some respect? Show me you care enough about me to give me assignments that push me beyond my limits. And don't let up on me even when I tell you I can't."

Engage, Excite, and Establish Expectations Strategy #29: Safe and Orderly

In the first generation of Larry Lezotte's now-famous *7 Correlates of Effective Schools*, he listed a *Safe and Orderly Environment* as the first correlate. Specifically, he wrote that effective schools have an "orderly, purposeful, businesslike atmosphere which is free from threat of physical harm. The school climate is not oppressive and is conducive to teaching and learning." Lezotte is clear that without the right environment, teachers can't teach and students can't learn at the levels necessary to drive achievement.

Having a school-wide behavior system or, in the least, very clear school-wide rules and expectations, is undoubtedly the starting point for any school. Some new principals are fortunate enough to inherit a school that is already *safe and orderly*. Statistically, the majority don't. Before any major real reform efforts will be successful, a school must have full control over student behaviors. That is why Lezotte started there, and that's why we start here in this chapter.

There is a tremendous amount of research on school-wide behavior management systems and discipline programs. I don't and won't endorse any specific ones here. You can find plenty online, from *Boys Town* to *Make Your Day*. Ultimately, much like a new reading program, any system or program can be highly effective with simplicity, fidelity, and consistency in implementation and maintenance.

Megan and I used the same behavior management system. It was one that she and her middle school team created during her time as a middle school teacher many years ago. They simply called it the *Passport* system. At CTS, we borrowed the *Passport*, made some modifications, and implemented it all three years. It continued after my time there. Many other schools in Phoenix now use the *Passport*, including Norma Jones School where Megan is now. As you'll see, there is nothing special or distinctive about the *Passport*. I'll briefly describe how it works below, and then I'll share the five reasons why it has been so effective in various schools.

The *Passport* is a simple piece of paper, half sheet or full sheet, that students are responsible for, not the teacher. In many ways, it works much like an actual passport – a student needs it to travel. It's a hall pass, a bathroom pass, an office pass. On the *Passport*, it lists the ten or so major behaviors that students are to avoid displaying – from bad language to missing a homework assignment to talking back to a teacher. Which behaviors are listed on the *Passport* depends upon the school's agreed-upon rules and expectations. Students get a new *Passport* every week and, throughout the week, students carry it everywhere they go. Their ultimate goal is to end the week with a *Perfect Passport*. Having a *Perfect Passport* comes with perks – dress down days, free homework passes, and so on.

Because we don't live in a perfect world, and because *zero tolerance* policies are harmful to kids, students can make up to two mistakes per week with no consequences. For example, they can miss a homework assignment on Tuesday and be tardy to 5th hour on Friday with no pomp and circumstance. They do lose their *Perfect Passport* privileges for the week, but they don't have any consequences.

Once a student gets a third or a fourth *mark* on their *Passport*, they receive a simple consequence such as lunch or after-school detention. If a student earns a fifth mark, they receive an office referral. At that point, it's up to administration what consequence is necessary. For students who struggle with behavior and exceed five marks, the progression starts over for students after the fifth mark. The sixth and seventh marks, much like the first and second, have no consequences and so on. Each week, no matter how bad the previous week was for particular students, every student starts fresh with a clean *Passport*.

The *Passport* system has a few other key rules and components such as what to do when a student loses his or her passport (on accident or on purpose), how behavior is tracked over time, and how to manage students who struggle, week after week, to maintain a *Perfect Passport*. I won't share those here because that's the not point of sharing the *Passport* system with you. The point of sharing it is because it teaches us five important lessons about school-wide behavior management systems, regardless of which system you ultimately choose to implement.

It Must Be Teacher-Friendly: Too many behavior management systems put all of the responsibility on teachers. Teachers must track points and marks. Teachers must oversee detentions. Teachers must be responsible for all parent communication. Teachers must input data into complex spreadsheets. Teachers must come to meetings ready to share their discipline data. With the way most discipline systems are created today, you'd think they are teacher behavior management systems.

It Must Be Student-Centered: Discipline systems must put the bulk of the responsibility on students. The *Passport* was highly effective because, once a teacher handed out the new *Passport* for the week, the teacher was essentially done. It was up to students to keep their *Passport*. It was up to students to behave well. It was up to students to monitor their own behavior. If a student broke a rule, the teacher (or any staff member) simply had to mark the *Passport*. The rest was on the student. The student knew that the third and fourth mark meant detention. It was up to him or her to attend detention (and serve the consequences if s/he didn't). If a student received a fifth mark, the teacher completed a very simple referral and could go back to teaching. Administration then handled the referral and the consequence.

All Staff Members Play an Equal Role: One of the greatest failures of most school-wide discipline systems is that the system only includes teachers and students. Teachers have more authority to monitor behavior than a crossing guard, a cafeteria worker, or a playground aide. With the *Passport*, every staff member had the same authority to mark a student's *Passport*. Of course, the point of the *Passport* wasn't to have adults everywhere looking for problems – we'll discuss that in the next section. But it was critical that every employee – from the principal to the PE teacher to the Parent Coordinator – had the same level of authorization on campus to monitor behavior and enforce expectations.

It Can't Be Solely Punitive: The *Passport* was highly effective not because it identified undesirable behaviors but because there was a big payoff for students who earned a *Perfect Passport*. *Perfect Passports* were like a status symbol. Although, day-to-day, students tried to avoid receiving marks, their ultimate goal was to try to earn dress down days and ice cream on Fridays (or whatever random rewards we'd give to students with

Perfect Passports). Remember, students love to work for and earn privileges and recognition.

It Can't Be Zero Tolerance: Discipline systems must allow students to make mistakes. Children are not, and cannot be expected to be, perfect day after day, week after week. They are human. The *Passport* allowed students to make up to two mistakes per week without any consequences. That's nearly 80 mistakes per year without having to serve detention or sit through a parent meeting explaining why they didn't complete their math homework.

Successful discipline systems must have a strong blend of consequences, incentives, and forgiveness. If they lean too heavily toward incentives then we are simply relying upon extrinsic motivation and not actually shaping behavior and developing responsible students. If we are too focused on consequences, then we are solely teaching students to avoid problems, not make good decisions.

That being said, there are definitely times when incentives and forgiveness aren't enough, and a principal needs to take control of a campus. In both schools that I took over, I had no choice but to make some really difficult and even controversial decisions that still hurt me to this day. As you've seen above, and as you'll see later in this chapter, I genuinely believe in forgiveness, second chances, learning experiences, and restoration. I'd want that for my own children. As leaders, in this day and age, when we know the research behind the *School-to-Prison Pipeline*, we have a moral obligation to keep our young men and women out of the legal system if at all possible. Every week, now that I serve as superintendent of nearly 30,000 students, I track discipline, suspension, and arrest data extremely closely to ensure that our school system is not contributing to the *pipeline*. It is critical that leaders do all they can to reduce suspensions and keep students in school when at all possible.

There were a times during my years as principal, however, that I had to take a bold stance to ensure the staff and students I was responsible for keeping safe were, in fact, safe.

Get Tough on Crime

It was the first day of a three-day Arizona Department of Education (ADE) visit. I had only been at Carl T. Smith for a short time – not long enough to make any major impact on behavior or achievement. We were still in survival mode. ADE was visiting because we were an *Underperforming* school, according to the state's labeling system at the time. I will always remember when the ADE official sat down with me to review our student achievement results. She opened her binder as we sat at a conference table. She looked down. Looked across the table at her colleague. She looked down again. "Wow," she said. "I honestly didn't know scores could go that low."

What she was alluding to was the fact that CTS only received six points on the state's labeling rubric. There were 28 total points a school could earn. It took 13 to become *Performing*. We weren't even halfway there. She made a joke that she thought schools got at least 10 points just for making sure their kids took the exam.

After we reviewed the data, and after being reminded again that I took over a school in crisis, she asked me what I liked about Carl T. Smith so far. I thought about it for a moment and then, for whatever reason, this comment came out of my mouth. "Well, what's great about middle school in general is that when we have problems, we have big problems. When I was at the elementary school, I navigated Hot Cheetos issues on the playground, 2nd graders who lost their pencils, and kindergartners who claimed their teachers didn't like them. Here, when I deal with a student issue, it's a drug issue or a fight or gang activity. In many ways, I'd prefer the major problems."

Literally, just as I finished commenting, Susana, the school secretary popped her head in the door with a panicked look on her face and motioned to me to come out immediately. I excused myself.

"Mr. G. Oh my God. You won't believe it. We just had a bomb threat. And I think it's real. About 30 seconds ago, I picked up the phone and ..."

Just then, the phone rang again. Susana freaked out and told the attendance clerk, Carla, to answer it. It was another bomb threat. Now Carla was in a panic. I took both of them back to my office to calm them down and, candidly, probably calm myself down. As we entered my office, the phone rang again. I had Carla run to the front and just transfer the call to my office. I picked up the phone.

"There is a bomb in your school. It is going to go off in the next 30 minutes. You must evacuate now if you want to save lives."

I hung up.

I hadn't been at the school long enough to even establish bomb threat procedures. Although we had discussed lockdown and evacuation expectations the week before school began, we hadn't practiced. I stood there in my office. I was 28. Three months ago I didn't want this job. Three months later, I still didn't want this job. At the moment, I really didn't want this job. I had ADE in the front office. I had hundreds of kids and a staff I had already grown to love sitting in classrooms that could potentially explode. I couldn't go on the intercom and announce there's a bomb in the building. That would create chaos. I couldn't run around from classroom to classroom to tell teachers individually. This was before text messaging. After a few minutes, I devised a plan.

First, I walked into the conference room. I sat down across the table from the ADE officials. I began, "So, you know how I was just telling you that when we have problems, we have big problems. Well, we've got a real big problem. We just

176

received three bomb threats and I have to evacuate the school. Although this isn't protocol, if I were you, I'd just take off now and go have a long, early lunch somewhere off campus. Come back in a couple of hours. By that time, we should have this figured out. Of course, you can stay, but we're about to evacuate to the parking lot and it's over 100 degrees outside."

Wisely, they quickly packed up and took off. I watched out the window as they got in their car and began to pull away. As soon as they reached the perimeter gate, I pulled the fire alarm. Over the next few minutes, hundreds of students and staff made their way out to the parking lot into the extreme heat. I huddled the staff outside to explain to them why we evacuated the school. Police were called and, within a few minutes, we had multiple police vehicles on campus. They even brought a bomb-sniffing dog. I walked the campus with law enforcement that day, going room to room, closet to closet, bathroom to bathroom. After about 30 minutes, they notified me that we were all clear and that students and staff could return.

On the way back in, a teacher stopped me to tell me that rumors were spreading fast that Adrian had called in the bomb threat from his cell phone in Ms. Peterson's room. As soon as she mentioned Adrian, I said to myself, "I should have thought of that a half hour ago before pulling the alarm!" You · see, Adrian was a known, dangerous gang-banger. He had been in system already for a few years – and he was only 15. He sold drugs, tagged neighborhoods, and instigated fights. He used the school as a marketplace to recruit gang members and push drugs. He wasn't there to learn. He was highly disruptive and would do anything, including call in a bomb threat, not to be in class.

To make a very long story short, we eventually found out, through student statements, that Adrian did call in the bomb threat from Ms. Peterson's room. But, as you could imagine, he had no plans to admit it. A police officer interrogated him for about 15 minutes, but once Adrian stopped answering questions, the officer had to stop.

"Sorry Mr. Principal. I can't do anything else. Even though we know it's him, I can't force him to admit it. You'll just have to administer some sort of discipline here at the school level. There's nothing we can do."

I paused for a moment, and then I asked the officer to make me a deal. "I know you can't interrogate him any longer, but I have all day. When I get him to admit, and I mean *when*, not *if*, I need you to promise me that you'll return here no later than 3:15PM. By 3:25PM, I need your car parked out front, lights flashing, and Adrian in handcuffs on the curb."

"Deal. But let me ask you, why 3:25PM?" he responded.

"That's because we dismiss at 3:30PM," I said. "I need every student and every parent in this school to know that, from this day forward, we mean business and that this campus will be safe for students, staff, and families."

Later that day, at 3:25PM, there sat Adrian on the curb as the dismissal bell rang.

A Few Bad Actors

With Adrian gone, the campus instantly became safer. Students who were scared of or controlled by him could now focus more on their work than their personal safety. At the time, I thought the removal of Adrian was all we needed to start to turn the ship, but I was wrong. As it turns out, after studying referral data and observing hallway, lunch time, and dismissal behaviors, I realized that there were three students – one in sixth, one in seventh, and one in eighth – who controlled the climate of campus. I knew that if I could manage, or even alternatively place, these three students, we could almost instantly make headway and begin to shift some of our energies away from behavior and instead to learning.

After several interventions, I felt I had no choice. I made a phone call to my superintendent. I explained the situation –

my perspective, my research, my current reality. I said to him, "I know that alternative placement is tricky. But if you want to see movement here at CTS, I actually can't have them on campus any more. If we can find a better placement for them, one that will better suit their personal needs, this will be my last ask of you during my entire tenure in this district."

He agreed. Within a few weeks, after discipline hearings and placement meetings, these three students were placed elsewhere, and, as harsh as this sounds, the rest is history.

A Public Proclamation

As a final example of having to go to extremes to create a safe and orderly campus, I once made a decision much bolder than the two aforementioned.

I had been principal at Camelback for a year and a half. We had made many significant changes, from establishing an advisory program to mandating club and sport involvement to improving counseling practices. Climate had tremendously improved. Culture was shifting. Working conditions were much better. But there was one major issue.

No matter how much we did, and no matter what programs and initiatives we implemented, there were about 150 students (150, not 4 like CTS) that had a strong grip on the climate and culture of the school. We had tried interventions, behavior modification, and counseling. Nothing was working. I came to a very sad realization that December, just a week or so before winter break. The realization was this: if I couldn't remove (yes, remove completely) at least 150 of the most dangerous and severely disruptive students, it didn't matter what I did, I would fail. And it wasn't about me failing – it was about the other 1,850 students who wanted so badly to come to a school that was safe, loving, supportive. At the time, those 150 students were much more powerful than the 225 staff members and the other 1,850 students.

For about 48 hours, I shouldered this burden all by myself. Then, a few days before the winter break, I asked my secretary to give me an hour in Camelback's TV studio to film a message that, if I didn't change my mind, I would show within the first few minutes that students returned in January. The video went something like this:

> "Good morning, students. I hope you had an amazing winter break. As you know, I have been the principal here at Camelback for a year and a half. I love it here. I wouldn't want to be anywhere else. In fact, virtually everywhere I go, I brag about you. I love you, I am so proud of you, and I am here to help you succeed no matter what the cost.
> Now I have to be honest. When I say that I brag about you everywhere I go, I am not talking about all of you. We have 2,000 students here. I am proud of about 1,850 of you. Unfortunately, there are about 150 students here at Camelback – and I know all 150 of you – that are making it impossible for the other 1,850 to thrive and excel here. It's not fair to them. Today marks a new day at Camelback. For many of you, today will be your last day at Camelback High School."

The video continued for a few more minutes. I explained that 20-25 students, over the next few days, would be removed from Camelback. I also explained that, for the rest of the 150, they had a choice: get on board with the new rules immediately or face removal.

For the next few months, as terrible as it sounds, we cleaned house. We made sure that, by the end of the school year, we had ridded Camelback of its 20-year gang and violence problem. And it worked. Throughout the remainder of that year, and in the coming years, students would randomly stop me to thank me. They said they had been bullied and beat up for years, and that they were finally safe.

Students would even write me letters at graduation thanking me for "kicking out the 150."

Here's the great news. Yes, believe it or not, there is great news in these stories. Once we had removed the four at CTS (Adrian and the three) as well as the 150 at Camelback, we were able to drastically reduce referrals, fights, and suspension rates. In fact, at CTS, we eventually moved to an all-in-school-suspension program and no longer suspended students out of school. We know that out-of-school suspensions directly contribute to the *school-to-prison pipeline*, and reducing time out of school should always be a major goal, even if that means you have to take drastic measures early to decrease suspensions later.

Engage, Excite, and Establish Expectations #30: Be Restorative

Earlier we read an excerpt from Larry Lezotte's first generation *7 Correlates of Effective Schools* where the primary focus was on minimizing or eliminating undesirable behaviors such as fights, disrespect, or drug use. Many years later, Lezotte authored a second generation *7 Correlates*. In this edition, he evolved away from an emphasis on reducing negative behaviors and instead to a focus on creating and sustaining positive learning environments where students are encouraged to help, collaborate, and interact with one another in productive ways.

The evolution of Lezotte's work around school discipline is indicative of a much bigger shift that has occurred over the years in education. Today, instead of implementing punitive systems to manage student behaviors, schools are encouraged to implement support systems that help students develop better decision-making skills and restore harm done to others. In no way does that mean that schools should abandon consequences and that school leaders should get soft on crime, so to speak, which is why we began this chapter with *safe and orderly*. Instead, leaders today need to adopt a much more *restorative* mindset when it comes to discipline.

The *Restorative Justice* movement that we are seeing around the country is a very important movement. I also don't believe it is the solution to all school-based issues. Rather, I do believe that it can serve as a much-improved perspective or framework for handing discipline at school. I will not get into detail in this book about *Restorative Justice* or *Restorative Practices*, as every school leader in America today should immerse him or herself in the literature. But I will share a couple brief thoughts and a couple stories to illustrate what *Restorative Justice,* as well as using *Restorative Practices*, looks and feels in schools today from a practical lens.

Suspensions Aren't Solutions

First of all, I am not opposed to suspensions. They have their place in the broad spectrum of school discipline techniques. Suspensions can be great for "cooling off." They can be effective in keeping kids separated after a fight or major altercation. They can also send a strong, clear message to other students that the school is serious about student behavior. But keep in mind that suspensions aren't solutions to bad behavior. Suspending a student for cursing at a teacher doesn't solve the profanity issue. Suspending a student for cheating on an exam doesn't solve the cheating issue or the student's lack of ethics. We must match consequences with learning and restoration. Students must learn from their mistakes, be taught how to make better decisions, and apologize for/restore the harm done to others. Suspensions in isolation are not effective.

An Eye for an Eye

This is one of the most inaccurately described Old

Testament verses in history. Many believe that the idea of an "eye for an eye" is simply that – if you poke my eye out, I'll poke your eye out. If you punch me, then I punch you. If you harm me, then I harm you. That's not what this verse was or is about by any measure. Instead, the meaning behind "eye for an eye" is that the punishment must match the crime. It doesn't mean that the punishment is the crime. This is a great lesson for school leaders today. If a student steals a pencil, the other student shouldn't steal their pencil. The student surely shouldn't be suspended for stealing either – that doesn't match the crime. As an alternative, they should have to apologize to the student from whom they stole the pencil and complete an hour of community service.

If a student gets in a fight at school, you don't kick them both out of school for weeks where they can fight on a daily basis in the community. Rather, you should coordinate a mediation and an apology. Each student should receive consequences that match the harm done to each other, which may include a short suspension to keep students separated for a couple days. Perhaps a research paper on why physical violence is not a solution to anger may be appropriate. Perhaps it's a presentation on the legal and personal implications of being charged with assault. Or it may be a Saturday of community service at the local food bank.

During an away game, several players from the girls volleyball team from Megan's school engaged in behaviors that were unacceptably disrespectful to the host school and their staff. One girl dropped her Gatorade bottle, spilling it all over the gym floor, and refused to clean it up. Another five became publicly disrespectful with the administrator on duty after the game. It was a horrible representation of their school and left Megan feeling embarrassed.

When the administrator on duty contacted Megan regarding the incident, her stomach sank. This was not something that happened at her school – they had already made great strides in student behavior and this was contrary to the Norma Jones way. She was disappointed with both her players and the coach. After considering the harm that had been done, Megan made the decision to assign consequences to the individuals and the team that were restorative, not punitive.

The individuals all had to call the other school's administrator to apologize and have a conversation about the impact of their behavior. They had to write letters to the other school to apologize for misrepresenting their school and not being respectful guests. In addition, the team had to forfeit their next game and use the time to perform community service on campus (transportation issues limited them from being able to go and perform community service at the other school). She never had a problem again with the volleyball team.

Megan uses restorative practices when handling general discipline issues as well. One great example was the way in which she dealt with a seventh grade boy, Carlos, who had earned several office referrals for being defiant and disrespectful in his classrooms. He was regularly disruptive and argumentative when he didn't want to do what was expected. Instead of off-campus suspension or the typical in-school-suspension, Megan assigned him a different on-campus task. She happened to have a kindergarten student, also named Carlos, who was constantly off-task. Megan walked seventh grade Carlos down to the kindergarten classroom and assigned him as a one-on-one aide to the kindergarten Carlos. He grumbled for a moment, but then sat right down on the carpet next to his new "friend." Each time Megan went in to check on him, he was actively engaged in helping kindergarten Carlos to learn how to follow directions and get his work done.

At some point during my first year at CTS, a sixth grade boy and his brothers snuck onto campus late one Sunday evening and tagged the entire school. The damage totaled over $20,000. We had security cameras, so determining who did the damage was the easy part. What discipline to administer was the challenge. The student had struggled greatly with behavior – disrespect, defiance, disruptions. This was a great chance to long-term suspend or even expel the student.

The insurance company needed a police report number to complete the claim, so police had to be notified. When law enforcement arrived, they asked if I wanted to press charges. Believe me, at the time, I was upset enough to press charges, especially considering how challenging this student had been on nearly a daily basis. I asked the officer how long I had to decide. He said that I could call him within the next couple of days with a decision.

I met with the entire family the next day. I found out that the parents were here on work visas and that the children, including the sixth grader, were undocumented. Pressing charges would mean deportation and the likely separation of the family. It would mean a complete and devastating lifestyle change. So, instead of charges, I decided to create a restoration plan. The student had to apologize to the entire student body and commit to excellent behavior moving forward. The family had to help repaint the school. That moment turned out to be a turning point for the young man. In fact, by his eighth grade year, he was chosen to speak at our final assembly. In that speech, in front of the entire school, he described CTS as a "sanctuary."

Engage, Excite, and Establish Expectations #31: Make Mountains Out of Molehills

As heartwarming as the sanctuary comment was, the goal of any behavior management system, or restorative approach to discipline, is to ultimately reduce the need for discipline altogether. Reducing suspensions is a great goal; reducing referrals and incidents is an ever better one. One of the ways in which I was able to reduce the overall numbers of referrals was because of the title of this Strategy – I always made *Mountains Out of Molehills*. If you want to avoid big problems, make the small problems feel big. If students know that not turning in homework is a major infraction at your school, then they wouldn't dare actually break a major rule.

If you want to stop tagging and etching in your bathrooms, make graffiti on personal property (binders and backpacks) a major campus infraction. If you want a clean campus at lunch time, make a huge deal about the one wrapper on the floor. If you want avoid bullying, (lovingly) lecture your students at the next assembly for not holding doors open for their classmates. If you want to avoid fights, make arguing in the hallway a mortal sin.

When I first learned that a local private college preparatory had a strict policy about hair length, I thought to myself, "That's a ridiculous rule. It's just hair. Let them grow it out. I can't believe that schools still fight over dress code and grooming." But after a conversation with one of their administrators, I found out this was a *Mountains Out of Molehills* policy. They believed that having a strict grooming policy sets a tone for other dress code and behavior policies.

Likewise, a sister high school district in Arizona has the strictest tardy policy I have ever heard of in my time in education. Their policy? If you are tardy to even one class, even if it's a random third period on a Thursday because your trip to the bathroom accidentally took too long, you receive an automatic half-day Saturday School. One tardy = half day on Saturday. I remember asking one of their principals about this policy. "How many staff members do you need here on Saturday to handle tardy detentions? I'd need to have 50 staff members and open up the gymnasium. Our tardiness is terrible."

He responded, "Oh we don't have a tardy problem. Saturday School is full of freshmen the first month of school until they figure it out. Otherwise, we just need one teacher here to supervise a small number of students."

After finishing the conversation, it dawned on me. This was another *Mountains Out of Molehills* policy. If students received 4 hours of weekend detention for being 5 seconds late to a class, there is no way they'd push the boundaries on other rules.

One of the biggest issues we had at CTS my first year was fights in the alleys and open properties before and after school. What was most troubling about this, aside from the fights and injuries, was the number of students who filmed the fights and posted them online. The worst part? Virtually every one of these fights was instigated by bystanders hoping to post a bloody battle online. I knew that my staff and I couldn't be everywhere before and after school, so stopping these fights was going to be nearly impossible. The only potential solution, I thought at the time, was to make filming and/or watching a fight a capital crime. So, I made a new *Mountains Out of Molehills* rule. The rule: anyone who is caught filming or watching a fight receives double the punishment of those involved in the fight. If the students received a two-day suspension, for example, then all those in attendance received four. If the students received 10 hours of community service, the bystanders received 20 hours.

As you can imagine, this wasn't a very popular policy with students or parents. But I also knew that it would probably only take a couple fights for people to know we meant business. Eventually, an after-school fight occurred. When we got our hands on the video, we were able to identify over ten students who stood around in a circle watching the fight. After determining the discipline for the fighters (three days), we called down the ten observers. And much to the dissatisfaction of students and parents, I suspended all ten kids for six days – and some were our Honor Roll students. But it was worth it. Believe it or not, that was the last community fight we had for the remainder of my time at CTS. It only took one *Molehill* to avoid an actual *Mountain*.

At this point, you are probably confused – or you think I am. At first, I said that leaders should get tough on crime and guarantee a safe and orderly campus at all costs. Then I said that leaders need to be restorative, avoid suspensions, don't contribute to the *school-to-prison pipeline*, and be thoughtful about consequences. And now I just told a story about suspending an Honor Roll kid for six days for watching a fight in a dirt lot 20 minutes after school. On one hand, this shows how complex school discipline is. There are times when a leader needs to be really tough to assure safety – set high expectations and stand by them at all costs. There are also times when a leader needs to take a stand against a particular issue – fighting, bullying, harassment. In these cases, harsh discipline may be necessary, especially the first year or two of a leader's tenure. However, when at all possible, a more restorative approach is ideal. We have to constantly remember that suspensions aren't solutions, and we must not become culpable of contributing to the *pipeline*. Either way, the primary goal of these Strategies is to reduce the number of infractions altogether to avoid discipline. The next Strategy is great example.

<u>E</u>ngage, Excite, and Establish Expectations #32: Lunch Matters

There is a popular leadership phrase that has been around for many years and has been used by a variety of leaders: "You can't fire your way to success." I think school discipline, in the long run, is the same. You can't suspend or expel your way to success. Granted, as I just mentioned, I felt very strongly at both CTS and Camelback that I had to take drastic measures to create safe and orderly campuses. However, that wasn't the case every year. Schools must be able to create strong systems and structures to guarantee safety and orderliness without a reliance upon suspensions. Aside from a school-wide behavior management system, like the *Passport* or *Boys Town* or *Make Your Day*, the next most important step to managing student behavior is having rock-solid lunch procedures.

Lunch behavior, if not controlled, can take up the vast majority of a school leader's time. Fights, injuries, theft, bullying, sexual assaults, and littering, to name a few, can become commonplace lunch activities without strong procedures and expectations. As an assistant principal, until I got a handle on it, I would spend well over 75% of my time dealing with the aftermath of lunchtime behavior. I would have to reschedule evaluations, miss leadership team meetings, and be late for parent events because I was dealing with lunch drama.

Over the years, both Megan and I have come up with eight steps to a better lunch. Although they do promote better structure and control, none of these include running militaristic lunches. In fact, as you'll see, one real key to a successful lunch is designing more positive and productive ways for students to engage with each other.

> **Shortened Lunch:** If at all possible, shorten your lunch period. When I got to CTS, lunch periods were 45 minutes. After one week of terrible lunchtime behavior, I shortened lunch to 27 minutes. Now, in hindsight, that was pretty drastic. But, the less time students have at lunch, the less problems you'll have. As a trade-off, in elementary school, tell your teachers they can have more recess time and, if at all possible, provide coverage for them.

> **Flipped Lunch:** Although Megan doesn't flip her lunches now, we did at CTS. Having kids play first and then eat second made a huge difference. By playing first, kids burn off energy, get hungrier, and come in to the cafeteria more tired. By eating last, kids

enter class more calm, more hydrated, and with much less noise and drama.

Cafeteria Procedures: There's no magic formula to perfect cafeteria rules. If there is magic, much like a school-wide discipline system, it's about simplicity, fidelity, and consistency. Here are a few suggestions to consider.

> **Seating Arrangements:** Consider making elementary school sit as a class and middle school students sit where they want – you'll avoid a lot of unnecessary drama letting teenagers sit with friends.
>
> **Quiet Tables:** Although this seems like it would only work in elementary, we always allowed the quietest tables to eat first and dismiss first. Loud tables were always last.
>
> **Cleanliness:** It must be a very clear expectation that the cafeteria is impeccably clean before students leave. If a student spills, they clean it, not the cafeteria staff. If a grade level somehow leaves the cafeteria a mess, call them all back to clean it up.
>
> **Cell Phones:** Although many schools still pick this battle, if you haven't already allowed cell phone usage at lunch, do it. You think it will cause more drama but, in all actuality, it makes for a much quieter and drama-free lunch.
>
> **Please and Thank You:** The cafeteria is the perfect place to teach manners. Every student

should say *please* if they ask for extras and *thank you* to the cafeteria staff for preparing and serving their food.

Close and Open Problem Areas: On every campus, there are problem areas. At CTS, it was the bathrooms. At Camelback, it was the handball courts. On your campus, it may be the gymnasium. Either way, make using those areas a privilege, not a right. If you have problems on the basketball courts one day, close it the next. If kids are caught smoking marijuana behind the handball courts, close the courts for a week.

Banish Bad Behaviors: Likewise, on virtually every campus, there are behaviors or activities that are problematic. At JB Sutton, it was Hot Cheetos and soda. At CTS, it was dodgeball (even though dodgeball eventually became a Friday favorite in P.E. class). At most elementary schools, it's tag. At some middle schools, it's a secret game of Truth or Dare. Don't be afraid to banish specific behaviors or activities. Make a public proclamation. Be swift and harsh with the first incident following the proclamation. Before you know it, that particular behavior will be history and you can move on to the next.

Promote Positive Activities: As the saying goes, "idle hands are the devil's workshop." If your school doesn't have a wide variety of engaging activities planned and available at lunch time, you are guaranteeing problems. Elementary school playgrounds should be full of jump ropes, balls, hula hoops, and other fun and interesting toys. Middle schools and high schools should have sports equipment, open gyms and weight rooms, open libraries and computer labs, and DJ's and informal dances in the courtyard on Fridays. Keep your students busy, and they'll stay out of trouble.

At Norma Jones, Megan partnered with a program called *Playworks* to provide her students with more structured, inclusive recess activities. Through this program, the school had a *Playworks Coach* on campus one week per month. The coach would work with each homeroom class to teach them fun playground games that they could engage in during recess. The school also had junior coaches, typically 5th graders, who came out during recess time to help lead games and keep track of the equipment for younger students. Students learned how to cooperate, include everyone, and communicate positively with each other. As a result, it was exceptionally rare that students were sent to the office for playground issues. And when I say rare, I mean that Megan now has less than five lunch time referrals per year.

Engage, Excite, and Establish Expectations #33: Know and Love Your Kids

The first time I stood in an assembly at Camelback and professed to a thousand students that I loved them, I had a few teachers tell me that they disagreed with my comments. A couple were even outright offended. One teacher caught me in a hallway a couple days after the assembly and had the audacity to say that love had no place in schools, especially high schools. "Telling kids you love them is not the right message, Dr. G. It's not even true. Love is a serious, personal emotion. We don't need more love in schools. We need more structure, more learning, and less emotion." For what it's worth, if you work in high schools, this comment probably won't surprise you.

Research says that there is a significant percentage of students in our classrooms today that do not hear the words,

"I love you." Their homes are so broken, their parents are so busy, or their lives are so chaotic that love doesn't find its way in as often as it should.

Merriam-Webster defines love as a "deep affection for one another; a warm attachment; an unselfish loyalty." In the most-used wedding scripture in America, 1 Corinthians 13 describes love in this way: "Love is patient, love is kind. It does not envy, it does not boast, it is not proud. It does not dishonor others, it is not self-seeking, it is not easily angered, it keeps no record of wrongs. Love does not delight in evil but rejoices with the truth. It always protects, always trusts, always hopes, always perseveres. Love never fails." I believe strongly that the foundation of healthy school culture – for both students and staff – is love.

For my remaining years at Camelback, I told our young men and women that I loved them every day. If I passed students in the hallways or in the library, I told them I loved them. In assemblies, video addresses, and guest teaching opportunities, I always ended with an "I love you" or a "we love you." Eventually, students began to say it back. One day, I was walking down the park because I had been told we may have an issue there. On my way, as I walked quickly down the sidewalk, a large group of students were making their way to the park on the other side of the road. When they saw me passing by, the whole group yelled in unison, "We love you, Dr. G." As awkward as it may have seemed, I yelled it back.

Eventually, love spread so much around campus that we added love to the annual climate survey. The question specifically was, "At Camelback, I feel loved." Students could select one of five options (from strongly disagree to strongly agree). By my last year at Camelback, nearly 90% of the students chose "agree" or "strongly agree" that they felt loved at school.

A few years after leaving Camelback, I was having a peaceful lunch in a local sandwich shop. As I was eating, a young man walked in. I originally didn't think much about it, as I only glanced up to see who walked in. From behind, it would have been easy to judge this young man. His pants seemed to defy gravity as they clung to his waist, his hoodie was much too big for his small frame, and the brim of his hat sat uncomfortably to the side. When he turned to sit down, he recognized me right away. "Hey, Dr. G! It's great to see you!" He gave me a big hug and talked about his community college courses, his job, and his friends that I remembered. I then gave him a quick update on me and my family. As we were wrapping up, he leaned in for another hug and, even though you would never guess that a young man looking the way he did that day would actually say in public, he ended with, "I love you, Dr. G."

One of the best and simplest ways in which you can show love for your student is to memorize as many names as possible. Even if you have 2,000 or 3,000 students in your school, you can make a concerted effort to memorize a few hundred. Start small by picking a couple major programs, clubs, or sports teams and memorize those names. For a few years, I would get a copy of the Student Government photo, write the first names of every student in the photo just below or above their face, and then work to memorize them. I was also very intentional about learning 2-3 new student names every week. I'd do this the first week of school all the way to the last week of school. Often, I'd memorize more than a few names per week. For me, the easiest way to memorize names of students was to learn 2-3 interesting facts about them. It was virtually impossible to memorize a random student's name, but if I knew that a student had six brothers, played volleyball, and went to Kennedy middle school, I was much more likely to memorize her name.

I recently attended a "Future 5th Grader Night" at my son's new middle school. A 7th grade student spoke that evening to share his journey at the school so far. I remember distinctly a

comment he made in his speech. He said, "My mom told me she believes that my true middle school
experience began when a teacher passed me in the hallway and called me by my name. I knew at that point I was a part of a community."

Engage, Excite, and Establish Expectations #34: Have (and Be) Fun

Being a principal is much like being a parent – you have to do more than just *say* I love you, you have to *show* it. Read any book on parenting, or even *Google* "How to be a good parent," and you'll find that the best parenting strategy is to show your kids you love them by spending quality time with them. This is not any different for school leaders today. Knowing students' names, telling them you love and care about them, and giving a high five, a fist pump, or a hug is a great start. But it's important that you go a step further.

Building relationships and engaging directly with students pays dividends in many ways. First, it makes the job of principal or school leader much more fulfilling. It's easy for principals to get mired down in the daily grind of managing the many challenges and problems of school leadership. Positive interactions with students is definitely a bucket filler. Second, it humanizes the school principal. Although decades ago it was important for the principal to be a revered and feared figure head that sat behind a large desk doling out discipline, students today want to know, love, and respect their principal, especially in middle and high schools. Finally, being known, loved, and respected by students makes it easier to implement new rules, new procedures, and even to administer discipline. When students buy-in to the principal, they buy in to rules and procedures on which they'd normally push back.

During my years at CTS and Camelback, I always intentionally made time to hang out with and play with students. I'd play basketball during lunch time, frisbee after school, foursquare before school, and hacky sack in the hallways. I would even dance on Fridays in the courtyard when the DJ came, and I'm terrible at dancing. I even once agreed to allow STUGO to turn the lights off in the middle of an assembly in the gymnasium so that I could sneak onto the middle of the basketball court to do the Harlem Shuffle. When the lights turned back on, there I was, the crazy guy in the middle of the court with no dance moves, dancing to a song I'd never heard of – and it didn't take but a few seconds for a ton of students to come join me.

While at CTS and Camelback, we also organized field days and homeroom (and advisory) competitions. Much like the Staff Olympics mentioned earlier, we would block off a couple hours on a Friday to get students engaged in fun, non-academic activities. Two of my most favorite memories occurred during homeroom/advisory competitions. At CTS, we asked every homeroom to create a class rap. They had to write and rehearse an original rap that would be performed, as a class, in front of the whole school. The winner would get a trophy to be displayed in their classroom. The students and teachers took this very seriously, and the performances were actually quite impressive … and hilarious. Imagine hundreds of "cool" middle school students acting like total dorks on stage as they performed in front of their peers. And imagine the sense of community this built and the impact it had on campus climate and culture.

My second favorite memory was at Camelback. With over 100 advisory classes and 2,000 students, organizing advisory competitions was quite challenging. Just wanting to start somewhere, I asked a group of students if they had any ideas. One student spoke out right away, "I know! Let's do a rock, paper, scissors competition. That way everyone has an equal chance at winning." Before long, we had organized a school-wide competition that began in every advisory. Each advisory had to have a rock, paper, scissors day to get down to one winner per advisory. Then, a couple days later, we organized a major school-wide advisory challenge where the 100 winners from each advisory competed against each other until we got down to the *Sweet 16*. Then, that next week, the *Sweet 16* competed against each other until we got down to 2 students.

To blow this way out of proportion, we decided to film the final two students in a live championship match that was aired in all advisory classrooms and offices (yes, Camelback had the capability of filming a live broadcast). We set up the bleachers so that we'd have some students in the audience. I did the color commentary. We set up a best-of-seven final round. We made those seven rounds as dramatic and long as possible. Finally, a winner emerged – a freshman who was largely unknown who instantly became popular. He was handed a trophy on live TV and gave a very awkward post-match interview. I mean, how do you answer the question, "So, what was your strategy?" He simply answered, "Well, I don't know. I just guessed every time."

Of all the ways I engaged and interacted with kids while I was at Camelback, the students were most appreciative of the times I joined them during clubs and sports. Although I never accomplished my goal, I originally set out to practice at least once with every sports team and participate in every club activity. I ran with the cross country teams, played hoops with the boys and girls, took batting practice with girls softball, and even participated in one football practice (non-contact of course). I was the guy in the dunk tank at the school carnival. I cooked with the culinary club. I (attempted) to build robots with the robotics club. My favorite activity of all time was acting in the school play. I agreed to play a role in a major production even though I don't have a theatrical bone in my body. I had to memorize lines, show up to rehearsals, and be there all three nights that we went live. I grew to appreciate the time, talent, and effort that goes into a performance and became (and still am) a huge advocate for the performing arts because of that experience.

Students love learning anything personal about teachers and principals. Think about how excited they get learning their teacher's first name. Sharing something personal (and appropriate) with students can help in building relationships with them, even as a principal. Megan decided to do this by sharing her love for the Seattle Seahawks. It started with her carrying her Seahawks coffee cup around with her all the time so that students would ask if she liked that team. It morphed into Megan sharing scores of games (if the Seahawks won) during morning announcements. Before long, students were approaching her to talk about football. She let them tease her when the Seahawks lost, and she quickly learned the teams for which her students pulled. She made sure to pay special attention to those teams' stats and players so that she could have an even better conversation with them the next time.

Megan also decided to add humor to every morning by sharing a daily joke during the announcements. She downloaded an app that provided her with a corny joke each day. It didn't take long before students were bringing her jokes to tell, and she often invited them up to tell the joke over the intercom. Students got so into this they began making up their own jokes to try to get on the announcements. Let's just say that some were better than others. Megan's favorite joke memory occurred around the holidays when she tried to tell a joke along the lines of: *What do you call an elf that wins the lottery? Welfy.* She lost it. While 500 students and staff listened, she laughed so hard she cried. It humanized her a little bit more, both with her kids and her colleagues.

Students vs. staff competitions were also a huge hit at Megan's school. At the end of a sports season, the school would host a staff vs. student game where the teams' players went head-to-head with the staff, including the principal. Students loved having the opportunity to try to beat their teachers and principal, and staff loved being able to show off hidden talents. Volleyball and softball were most popular, as not as many staff members were willing to play soccer, as that requires too much running.

This goes without saying, but it is not only important to engage with students in fun and exciting ways, it's also important to attend their events. In chapter 6, I talked about the importance of *Attend Everything*. Attending events is not only a good intelligence-gathering tactic, it's a wise investment of time. I once had a veteran teacher tell me that the number one middle school and high school classroom management strategy is event attendance. He once told me during a football game, "If you want to have excellent classroom management, go to all of your students' sporting events and club activities. When they see you there, they know you care. And when they know you care, they won't mess with you in class. They will also make sure their peers don't mess with you either." This rule also applies to school leaders.

Engage, Excite, and Establish Expectations #35: Make Success Mandatory

There's a comic strip that has been around for a few years now that humorously (yet accurately) portrays a typical parent's reaction to a bad report card in the 1960's compared to the most common reaction in 2010. As you can guess, in the 1960s, a bad report card was the child's fault. Parents wouldn't even think about blaming the teacher or the school. Bad grades were the result of a lack of effort, not bad teaching. But fast-forward 50 years and bad report cards are almost entirely the teacher's fault – they went too fast or too slow, they didn't modify or accommodate enough, they weren't patient enough, they were too rigorous. For some reason, in this modern era of education, we put all of the pressure and accountability on teachers, not kids, to be successful.

If we want to improve student achievement in schools

today, we need to look to the kids just as much as we do the teachers. The daily objective of leadership shouldn't be to get teachers to work harder but rather to make kids work harder. The accountability, the pressure, and the high expectations that teachers feel should also be felt by students. Leaders can and should create a healthy sense of accountability for students by developing systems and structures that increase rigor and expectations for students, all while providing the support necessary for all students to be successful.

At Carl T. Smith, we made success mandatory by implementing what we called *Exit Criteria*. Instead of simply passing students from grade level to grade level regardless of achievement or mastery, we created a very clear set of skills, competencies, and projects for each grade level that students had to master or complete in order to promote to the next grade level. If a student fell short in one area, they could pass to the next grade level but had to re-take that particular class the next year during one of their electives (special areas). For example, if a student completed her sixth grade *Exit Criteria* in all content areas other than science, she would promote to the seventh grade but would take science during her PE class the next year. If a student failed in more than one area, s/he was held back a year. Truth is, because of the support structures we put in place, very few kids were retained.

I will not list the *Exit Criteria* for all grade levels here in this book because your teams should determine the best *Exit Criteria* for your school based on your goals, curriculum, and programs. I will share our fifth grade *Criteria* below as an example. What you'll see is that the *Criteria* is a mix of skills, competencies, and projects. What you'll also notice is that state assessments were not a part of *Exit Criteria*.

> **Reading:** Read the five books assigned to each student. At a minimum, every student at CTS had to read the number of books that matched their grade level (five books in fifth grade, six books in sixth grade, and so

on). Not every student read the same books, as books were assigned based on reading level.

English: Successfully pass both semester benchmark exams.

Math: Successfully pass both semester benchmark exams.

Science: Successfully complete a Science Fair project and effectively present the project at the school-wide fair.

Social Studies: Successfully complete both semester essays.

Special Areas (Art, Technology, PE, Health): Each elective teacher created his or her own *Criteria* that ranged from running a mile within a specified amount of time to completing three art pieces.

Teachers were responsible for tracking progress toward these goals so that there were no surprises at the end of the year. For example, if a reading teacher knew that Jose hadn't even completed one book by January, that teacher needed to put a plan in place to get the student on track. It was the student's responsibility to follow the plan, but the teacher had to help develop it. Additionally, at the end of each semester, after benchmark exams were completed and essays were turned in, teachers organized after-school and weekend tutoring and make-up exams for students who failed. Students had to come in after-school and on weekends until they passed. The same occurred at the end of the year. Students who did not pass or complete their *Exit Criteria* had to attend summer school in order to promote to the next grade level. Failure wasn't optional.

At Camelback, when I found out that we had 800 more students failing classes than we had who qualified for Honor Roll (a story you'll hear in the next Strategy), I knew we needed a multi-pronged approach to solving this issue. First, we needed more consistent and strategic grade tracking. Second, we needed to launch a robust Honor Roll program to promote achievement. Third, we needed a comprehensive tutoring and support program to intervene early and often. Grade tracking was simple – we moved to a 3-week progress report system at which point all students would have a grade-check by their advisor during the advisory period. The Honor Roll system is the topic of the next Strategy.

As for the comprehensive intervention program, we launched Success Is Mandatory, or SIM. SIM had multiple components, all designed to increase support, remove barriers and excuses, and decrease failure rates. Below are the major components.

> **Mandatory Tutoring Hours:** Every student who had multiple D's or failed one or more classes in a particular quarter was assigned mandatory tutoring hours. Students who had multiple D's or one F had to complete 10 hours of tutoring the quarter following the grading term. Students who had two F's were required to complete 20 hours. Students who had 3 or more F's were required to complete 30 hours of tutoring.

> **Tutoring Around the Clock:** To remove barriers and excuses, we offered tutoring around the clock. Students could receive tutoring before school, during advisory, during lunch, after school, and on Saturdays.

> **Open Library:** The library at Camelback opened every day no later than 7:00AM. It remained open until 5:30PM. It was also open on Saturdays for at least four hours.

Teacher Tutoring: Teachers were available every advisory period, after school in the library, and Saturdays to assist students with make-up exams, tutoring, test prep, or even just homework.

Peer Tutoring: The vast majority of the tutoring on campus was done through a peer tutoring program. The program was loosely based off of Peer Power ™ in Memphis, Tennessee, a program I mentioned in Chapter 8. I say loosely because their program was based on peer tutoring teams and used a point system/competition to drive outcomes – Camelback's was not. Peer tutors were available in the library before, during, and after school as well as Saturdays. The tutoring program was led by approximately 10 lead tutors, all of whom were paid small scholarships for their time and effort. The remaining tutors earned community service hours.

Learning Labs: For more intensive tutoring, certain students were assigned to "learning labs" during Advisory and Saturdays in which we placed some of our strongest teachers to help students fill learning gaps in English and math.

Every three weeks, advisors checked students' grades and tutoring hours to make sure they were on track. Students who were not on track had to meet with their assigned administrator (we divided the school into "Advisory Strands" in which each administrator oversaw approximately 300 students and 20 advisories to enhance support and accountability for students).

Like many schools, Megan's school struggled to get students to complete homework. Teachers were frustrated trying to find ways to hold students accountable – their district had a standards-based grading system that didn't allow students' grades to be penalized for incomplete work. During a summer leadership retreat, Megan's Cabinets were meeting jointly to discuss the issue of homework. They knew that one of the root causes had to do with students not having a consistent place, free of distractions, to complete homework.

They also decided to look at the problem from a lens of presuming positive intentions – a norm of collaboration they followed. The teams decided that they needed to assume that all students *wanted* to meet the homework expectation but had a valid reason for not completing homework. Therefore, they needed to provide students with the structure and time to complete missing work. Any time students missed an assignment, they had the "mandatory privilege" of going to a classroom during lunchtime to complete their work. If they missed two or more assignments in a week, they had the "mandatory privilege" of going to the after-school Homework Help room. Some students had this privilege assigned indefinitely.

Another major issue for most schools is end-of-year behavior and focus of students. Usually, the end of the 8th grade year (or 5th grade in elementary schools or 12th grade in high schools) can be even difficult for both staff and students. Students begin to mentally check out, which often leads to an increase in unwanted behaviors and a decrease in quality work. This is especially true for seniors (*senioritis*). For Megan, in an effort to make the end of 8th grade special yet hold students accountable, Megan's school implemented *End of Year Contracts* for the final quarter of school. The junior high teachers plan out multiple incentives and activities, including field trips, class competitions, free dress for the month of May, and finally, 8th grade promotion. Students and parents sign a contract that states that students will meet expectations for work, attendance, and behavior. Each time they fail to meet the expectations, they lose a privilege on their contract. The contracts had such a positive impact, the team decided to include 7th graders as well. Contracts have turned out to be a perfect blend of incentives and consequences, and Norma Jones does not struggle with negative end-of-year behaviors like many other schools.

Making success mandatory, whether through programs or initiatives like Exit Criteria, Homework Help, Contracts, or SIM, is not just about holding students accountable, it's about removing barriers and providing the appropriate levels of supports to ensure all students succeed. But schools, and the students within them, can't just pursue reduced failure – they must also pursue increased academic achievement.

Engage, Excite, and Establish Expectations Strategy #36: Make It Cool to Be Smart

One of my favorite authors is Malcolm Gladwell. If you haven't read any of his books, you should buy a few copies for your next vacation. My favorites are still *Outliers* and *Blink*. The first Gladwell book I ever read was *Tipping Point*. In this book, he makes a strong case that little things can make a big difference in a social or organizational context. One example he used was crime in New York City, where he (and many others) have attributed the drastic decrease in crime in New York in the 1990s to a graffiti removal program. As the City removed graffiti from the subways, it also removed crime. The cleaner the City, the safer it became. New York didn't have to invest large sums of money into more officers or programs. Simply, they needed to reduce graffiti to create a tipping point in the city.

I have argued for many years that there is a "tipping point" in schools, much like graffiti in cities or *likes* on social media. The tipping point is simply this – when it's cooler to be smart than it is to be bad, then your school has made it. When the *cool* kids are the *bad* kids, you have tough work ahead of you. When the cool kids are the good kids, you are poised to experience major academic gains. Of course, as you can probably guess, I would never actually label kids "bad" or "good." I am simply making a point here. In elementary schools, it's often the class clowns that are the most popular. In middle schools, it's the troublemakers. In high schools, it's often the star athletes. The bad news is – we are to blame. The good news is – you have the power to change it.

The reason why athletes are most popular in high schools is because we do pep rallies for sports but not pep rallies for academics. The reason why class clowns get the most attention in elementary school is because we give them the most attention. The reason why the "bad boys" are the coolest in middle school is because teachers and administrators talk about them all the time. If you want to create a tipping point in your school, where it's cooler to be smart than it is to be athletic or mischievous, then stop doing what we've always done in schools.

Before moving on, it is important to note that when I say "*Make It Cool to Be Smart*," I don't actually mean *smart*. What I mean is good, well-behaved, hard-working, or respectful. Ultimately, "be smart" is a placeholder for any attitude, behavior, or outcome that you want students to display day-to-day on your campus.

Honor Roll

Even if your school already has an Honor Roll, you should re-think it. Most schools have an Honor Roll that has such a high bar that only the top ten percenters can attain it. It doesn't help your school culture to only give academic awards to the Top 10%. You need to make Honor Roll attainable, through hard work, for the average student. You need a much larger Honor Roll – one that recognizes and honors the top 25%, 33%, or even 50%. At CTS, we had three levels of Honor Roll. We had *Principal's Honor Roll* which was for the top ten percenters. Then we had *Honor Roll* which was for the next 15 or so percent of students. Then we had *Academic Honorable*

Mention. These were definitely not the top 10 or 25 percenters, but they were kids who were working hard and making great improvements. Sometimes, we'd sneak a young man or woman onto the *Academic Honorable Mention* as an encouragement, even if they didn't quite meet the criteria.

Near-Perfect Attendance

One of the best ways to encourage good attendance is to recognize it. The only problem with most attendance programs is that it only recognizes those with perfect attendance. Truth is, what most principals want is not perfect attendance but excellent attendance. Those are two different things. If a student misses one (or even two) days per quarter or semester, that's excellent attendance and will lead to better learning. So, make a slight shift to your attendance program. Instead of *Perfect Attendance* awards, start giving out *Exemplary Attendance* awards and you'll see your attendance improve.

Student of the Month

What's great about the Student of the Month is that it doesn't have to go to an academic high flier. Students of the Month can go to anyone. Remember – you are trying to create a tipping point. Student of the Month can be students who are showing improvement. It can be students who had a terrible start to the school year and have made a tremendous turnaround. It may be a troublemaker who, even though he or she isn't quite exemplary, finally had a good month. It may even go to a student that is so quiet and shy that no one knows them. Use Student of the Month wisely, especially if you have an expanded Honor Roll program.

And the Attention Goes to ...

The key to creating a cultural tipping point is not the awards themselves. The key is the recognition and the perks. First, I'll briefly cover the recognition. Student of the Month, Honor Roll, and Exemplary Attendance awards must be given in front of the whole school. They can't be reserved for a "by invite only" assembly or an evening event for just parents. Those are fine – you can do those as well. But if you want to *Make It Cool to Be Smart*, you have to dedicate the time to do it in front of everyone. At CTS, since we had an assembly virtually every Friday, this was very easy to do. If you don't have set assemblies (which I'll try to convince you to do in the next Strategy), you need to create achievement assemblies.

At Camelback, we had what we called *Academic Achievement Awards Assemblies*. It was an academic pep rally on steroids where, in front of the whole school, we recognized as many students as we could. We had Spartan SHIELD awards, Most Improved awards, ACT and SAT awards, scholarship awards, department awards, and so on. We interviewed a few outstanding students ahead of time and created video vignettes of those interviews that were played throughout the assembly. Students in the audience cheered for academic achievement just as loudly and proudly as they did athletes who won the division championship. The goal was always two-fold: (a) recognize students for their hard work and accomplishments and (b) *Make It Cool to Be Smart*.

When Megan's school rolled out their school-wide expectations of being *Polite, Prepared, and Punctual*, otherwise known as *The 3Ps*, they decided to immediately develop a way of recognizing students who met those expectations. The school had historically recognized students for Honor Roll and Exemplary Attendance, but that was it. At the beginning of the second month of school they held their first-ever *First Friday Assembly*. During this assembly, each teacher recognized one student from their class who earned *The 3Ps* award in front of their peers. Not only did this give students a chance to be recognized for something non-academic, but they knew the clear criteria for how to earn the award. This also gave teachers the opportunity to recognize "struggling" students who had made improvements, which provided further encouragement for them to stay on the right track.

And the Perks Go to ...

Recognition is the just the beginning. Where you will get your biggest bang for the buck is in giving perks to students who earn Honor Roll, Student of the Month, and Exemplary Attendance. You want to make these status symbols on campus. Just as the best athlete used to be the *big (wo)man* on campus, you want to make the nerdy, chess-playing, Math Olympiad the new Lebron James or Serena Williams. Perks can be simple like the ones at Norma Jones. One example at Norma Jones is that students who earn Honor Roll during the school year are eligible to go on an end-of-the-year field trip to a local skating rink. This has become one of the most exciting and desired events of the year. Another example is that students who had a "clean" STAR Card (their version of the *Perfect Passport* mentioned earlier) for the week got to wear free dress the following Monday (Jones is also a uniform school). To give you a more in-depth look as to how to truly *Make It Cool to Be Smart*, here is a glimpse into what this looked like at CTS and Camelback.

Carl T. Smith

Students at CTS were required to wear uniforms. Middle school students hate uniforms and would do virtually anything not to have to wear them. Every week, there were three opportunities to have a "dress down." Every student who had a *Perfect Passport* the week before was entitled to dress down on Friday. Every student who earned Honor

Roll for the quarter earned the privilege to dress down every Monday for the entire next quarter (1st quarter Honor Roll = 2nd quarter dress down on Mondays). Finally, every student who earned Exemplary Attendance for the quarter could dress down every Tuesday for the entire next quarter (2nd quarter Exemplary Attendance = 3rd quarter dress down on Tuesdays). If you were a hard-working, well-behaved, regularly-attending scholar (we called them scholars, not students), you would get three dress down days per week. Now that's cool.

Dress down wasn't the only perk. Honor Roll students ate lunch first. Every day, after a few minutes outside, grade levels would make their way into the cafeteria and have a seat. As per *Lunch Matters*, they could sit wherever they wanted. Once the cafeteria was settled, someone (cafeteria staff, the assistant principal, or myself) would yell, "Honor Roll." At that moment, all of the Honor Roll students would get up to get in line first. The rest had to stay in their seats until Honor Roll was done being served, then we'd dismiss the rest of the tables, starting with the quietest table.

There were two other perks to being on Honor Roll. A handful of times per year, just to make Honor Roll more special, I would order popsicles or ice cream sandwiches through Food Services. Then, about 5 minutes before dismissal on a Friday, I would make an *all call*, "Good afternoon CTS! Can I please have all Honor Roll students pack up a few minutes early today and come to the cafeteria for free ice cream." The other major benefit to being on Honor Roll was free admission to dances. Although we didn't have many dances, they were very popular. Honor Roll students always got in free and always got in first.

Camelback

At Camelback, we took this idea of *Make It Cool to Be Smart* to a different level. After spending time listening to and learning from students through various venues (described in previous chapters), I concluded that two of the most common complaints about Camelback were (a) the lunch lines were too long and (b) the fact that once a student took his or her ID photo their freshman year, they never got to take it again – they were stuck with their awkward freshman year picture all four years. So, I decided to make these the starting places for Honor Roll. But, first, we had to establish an Honor Roll.

Earlier in this book, I talked about the first time I had our office staff run me a report on the number of students who were failing one or more classes – almost 1,100 out of 1,900 at the time. What I didn't mention earlier is that I also asked the front office to run me a report on the number of students who were on the Honor Roll. Their response? "Honor Roll? What Honor Roll?"

I had them run for me a hypothetical Honor Roll. I gave them parameters for what I thought Honor Roll would be – a minimum GPA and no Ds or Fs. The total? 300 out of 1,900. We had an 800 student difference (in the wrong direction) between those failing and those qualifying for Honor Roll (1,100 versus 300). At that moment, I created an ambitious goal. I proclaimed that we would start a robust Honor Roll program and that within four semesters, we would have more students on Honor Roll than we had failing one or more classes. Believe it or not, it took only two semesters. By the time we calculated Honor Roll and the failure list two semesters later, we had 600 students on Honor Roll and 550 students failing one or more classes. How did we do this?

First, we created Success Is Mandatory to give every student a path to success through accountability and support described earlier in this chapter. Second, we decided to take Honor Roll to a whole new level. We created a special ID that only Honor Roll students could have. We made the normal ID that all students had to wear as plain and boring as possible. The Honor Roll IDs, on the other hand, were incredible. They were created by our digital design students, and they were artistic and very unique. Every semester, we would hand out Honor Roll certificates to all students who qualified in front of their peers, and then they could go to the bookstore to get their new IDs. With the new IDs, however, came with a special perk – they could take a new picture. The couple days after Honor Roll certificates were handed out, the bookstore had long lines of excited students getting a new picture. The best part? There was a huge percentage of students who wouldn't *cash in* on their new ID and new photo for a couple of days so that they could go get a new haircut, style, or color at a salon so that their ID photo was perfect. That's how *cool* it was to get a new picture .. and to be on Honor Roll.

We didn't stop there (although, to be candid, the cool ID with a new picture was probably enough). The ID gave students special privileges – three to be exact. The big picture idea was to make Honor Roll ID's "all access passes" to privileges. The first was lunch. All students with an Honor Roll ID were dismissed about 3 minutes early every day for lunch so that they could be the first in line. The second privilege was access to the game room I mentioned earlier in the *Community Network* Strategy. Only students who had an Honor Roll ID could use the room during lunch. The third and final major perk of the ID was free admissions to all sporting events (and reduced pricing on dances). Imagine a line of students waiting to pay to get into the football game on Friday. And then imagine another quick access point where a bunch of Honor Roll students quickly walked into the game as they flashed their fancy ID's and said, "I'm on the Honor Roll."

Engage, Excite, and Establish Expectations #37: Bring Back the Assembly

Every summer, the Harvard Graduate School of Education, HGSE, hosts a series of week-long summer workshops for practitioners. In the summer of 2006, I attended their *Urban*

School Leaders Institute. It was an amazing week of networking and learning, and I left Boston much more energized and motivated to transform Carl T. Smith than I was before I made the trip. After nearly 5 days of speakers and presentations, it was finally time for the last speaker – an unassuming, aging woman who was a retired principal from Brooklyn. Most of the speakers before her were well-known researchers – they were highly intelligent, inspirational, and insightful. But here she was, a frail-looking woman in her late-70's to early 80's, who wasn't a famous Harvard researcher. She was *just* a practitioner – and she was, by far, the most memorable. I can still quote her today without referencing any notes or journals – and this was twelve years ago.

Of all of the nuggets that she shared, one stuck with me the most. In fact, it's the title of this Strategy. Over a decade ago, she stood there on the lecture stage, paused for a moment, looked around the room, and said so confidently, "I know you've heard from a bunch of incredible speakers this week. I have been fortunate to learn from most of them. I know they have given you tremendous insights that you plan to use back on your campuses. But I want you to remember what I'm about to tell you. In fact, if you don't remember anything else this entire week, remember this. It's time to *Bring Back the Assembly.* The only way to truly build school culture is through gathering all your people in one room at the same time and being crazy together." I immediately drank the Kool Aid.

Typically, I caution school leaders that the worst thing they can do is fly to a fancy summer conference, learn new ideas, and come back and implement them right away without planning, collaboration, and alignment to a broader vision. However, this one time, I have to admit I was that guy. I was convinced in that very moment that she was right, and I instantly knew how and when we would do assemblies. As crazy as it sounds, I decided to host weekly school-wide assemblies right in the middle of the reading block. You know, that sacred time that no-one is ever allowed to interrupt? Well, I decided that we'd interrupt it every Friday. At the time, the teachers hated the idea. I didn't care. I knew it was the right way to really start to create the culture and climate we wanted and everyone on campus deserved.

So, that next August, we began our weekly assemblies. Our assemblies were simple, most less than 10 minutes. Others lasted 20-30 minutes depending on the agenda. We used no PowerPoints, Prezis, or Keynotes. We just came together once a week to be crazy together. To show you how simple these assemblies were to organize, here were our procedures.

> Every time, every class sat in the same place. We didn't have a gym or an auditorium – we just had a small "cafetorium." That meant that everyone had to sit on the floor. The school (the staff and students) learned that they had to come in fast, sit in their assigned areas, and get ready within a couple of minutes.

> Once everyone was seated, we began with our school wide chant (we'll talk about that in the next *Strategy*). To begin, the entire school would do the chant. Then we'd go grade level by grade level to see who was the loudest. Fifth grade would go first, then sixth, then seventh, and then eighth. Upper grades weren't allowed to boo – this was about building school culture and a stronger sense of community. To mix it up, sometimes we'd do boys versus girls. Other times we'd have fifth and sixth grades say the first part and seventh and eighth chant the second part.

> Then every student who had a birthday that week had to stand up. Even if a student didn't want to stand up, their friends made them stand up. Then the entire

school sang happy birthday to them the CTS way. It was a specific way. If they did it wrong, we'd stop the song, laugh about it, and do it over until we got it right.

Then we'd do the same for the staff – if any staff members had a birthday, we'd sing to them the CTS way.

Then, if we didn't' have anything important to do, I'd make a couple small announcements, try to say something funny or inspirational, lecture about a piece of paper I saw on the ground in the bathroom (*Make Mountains Out of Molehills*), and send them back to class.

We did often use assemblies for much more than chants and birthday songs. Assemblies were the perfect place to recognize Honor Roll and Exemplary Attendance students. We would announce Students of the Month during this time. We would celebrate sports and other academic championships (district Spelling Bee, Science Fair, etc.). In addition, if we ever had to address serious issues – an incident in the community, a change in a major policy or procedure, preparation for the state exam or eighth grade promotion – we would use this time.

As mentioned earlier, Megan's school started hosting *First Friday Assemblies* (one for Kinder-4th grade and one for 5th-8th grade) at the beginning of each month. During the assembly, *The 3Ps* winners were recognized, the PE coach would lead fun competitions between students and staff, and birthdays were celebrated. The assemblies always started with the school cheer, led by student ambassadors. One of the most entertaining parts of the assemblies happened right after the school cheer: Roll Call. Each class, from kindergartens to 8th graders would be called upon to do their cheer. The younger grades usually kept the same cheer each time, but the 6th-8th grade classes ramped it up. They wrote new chants, sometimes raps complete with music, that they performed. Students you would never expect were courageous enough to come up in front of everyone, grab the microphone, and lead their class. The competition was always friendly, with classes all claiming they were smarter than the next or would perform better on the upcoming state assessment.

When I arrived at Camelback, like most high schools, we already had a structure in place for pep rallies and sport assemblies like Homecoming. They had 4 assemblies a year, on average one per quarter. I was warned by many staff members that student behavior in assemblies was terrible and that one time, one of the many previous principals tried to host an assembly in the football stadium, and when it ended, students just went home instead of going back to class. It was mid-day. I already had a taste for bad assembly behavior at Camelback. During the "Future Freshman" assembly that summer before school began, the attitudes, respect level, and overall behavior of the incoming freshmen was horrible – offensive at best. I had to have staff members remove students I had never met from the audience just so I could finish the assembly. I still remember how frustrating that was.

Despite that failed assembly, I moved forward with plans to host an assembly the first Friday of school to set the tone for my time at Camelback. I wanted to introduce myself, talk about some general expectations, and deliver a message about the importance of a quality education. The staff thought I was crazy: "These kids can't behave for a 30-minute assembly that has nothing to do with sports or entertainment." Regardless, I felt strongly then, and still do today, that it is essential that principals set the tone for the year through a week one (or week two) assembly. I hosted them at CTS all three years and at Camelback all five years. In fact, eventually at Camelback, we hosted five assemblies to start the year – a whole-school assembly, a senior assembly, a junior assembly, a sophomore assembly, and a freshmen assembly. Having grade level assemblies allowed our team to tailor messages to each grade level – for seniors, for example, the focus was on college and finishing strong.

As for that first assembly at Camelback, it was a great success. The students weren't perfectly behaved, but they were respectful and quiet when they needed to be. Taking the advice of the staff, I made the message much more student-friendly and entertaining. I did use the time to introduce myself and discuss new expectations. But I used most of the time, through pictures, stories, and statistics, to share with students why graduating from high school and college was a much better option in life than dropping out (at the time, we still had a graduation and dropout problem). Ultimately, the message was that college was within reach for anyone who wanted it, and that we were committed to helping any and every student realize their dreams. At the end of the assembly, the Senior Class President came up to me, tears in her eyes, and said, "My life would have been much different if I had heard that message four years ago. I am inspired to have an amazing senior year." That's the power of assemblies.

Throughout my time at Camelback, we hosted many different types of assemblies, all with different goals and purposes.

> **Welcome Back:** As mentioned above, I began every year as a principal with a school-wide assembly the first week of school to set the tone, share new expectations, and deliver an inspirational message.
>
> **Grade Level:** Also as previously mentioned, grade level assemblies are a strategic way to customize messages. Grade level assemblies are also great ways to start the second semester.

Guest Speakers: When I had the opportunity to bring an inspirational speaker to Camelback, I did. Whether it was a nuclear engineer or community member with an inspiring story, I believed that if an assembly changed even one life, it was worth it.

College and Career: Whether it was Career Day, a speaker from the local university talking about admissions requirements, or an informational session about scholarships, getting freshmen off to a good start and seniors to finish strong was always a value-add to the lives of our students.

Life Lessons: There were a few instances when we hosted assemblies that had specific lessons and messages that we believed our students needed to hear. We hosted Rachel's Challenge ™, an anti-bullying assembly. After that major car accident my second year that I mentioned earlier, we hosted a driving safety assembly. Before prom, in partnership with the City of Phoenix, we hosted a "mock crash" assembly where students were able to witness and experience the drama and trauma of the scene of a car accident that was the result of underage drinking.

Sports: Although I may have downplayed the importance of student-athletes earlier, I happened to be one myself throughout school and am very supportive of athletics. Sports assemblies are great ways to build pride in the school and recognize talented students.

Arts: Instead of relinquishing major theatre and dance productions to evening showings for parents, we often offered matinee performances during the day to promote the arts and encourage students to attend the evening events.

Academic Achievement: As you read about in the previous *Strategy*, our academic achievement assemblies played a major role in making it *Cool to Be Smart*.

Graduation: If you run a middle school or a high school, promotion and graduation ceremonies take a tremendous amount of coordination and communication. We never hesitated to host assemblies to review expectations and share important information.

One final point about the importance of hosting quality and engaging assemblies. I remember one of the first sports and entertainment assemblies I ever attended at Camelback. These were entirely run by STUGO. I rarely had a speaking role. Other than sports coaches introducing their teams, staff didn't have speaking roles either. This particular assembly wasn't as organized or engaging as the others, and the students in the audience became a little restless. They weren't poorly behaved, they just weren't perfectly quiet when they were supposed to be (National Anthem, introductions of teams). When one of the coaches began to introduce her team, she became very upset that students didn't get quiet enough. So then she began to yell at them through the microphone. And when I mean yell at them, I mean yell.

It was so bad, I had to walk onto the court, make my way over to her as she continued to yell at the students, and attempted to take the microphone from her. And you wouldn't believe what she did – she began to yell at me. In front of the entire school. And when she was done yelling at me, instead of handing me the microphone, she threw it. Thank God a student with great hand-eye coordination was in the area and caught it. She stormed off the court, through the students, and then slammed the door as hard as she could as she left the gym.

The end of that story is too long to tell, but here is the point. Regardless of the type of assembly, it is essential that assemblies are fun, engaging, humorous, relevant, and/or inspirational. Assemblies are supposed to help improve culture, climate, relationships, work ethic, and behavior. When assemblies are boring, unengaging, and/or un-inspirational, students will lose interest quickly. Just as you need to create expectations for student behavior during assemblies, you also need to create expectations for the level of engagement and the relevance of the content for assemblies so they fulfill the intended outcome.

Engage, Excite, and Establish Expectations #38: Create a School Chant or Slogan

It was a few months into my first year at CTS before we created a school chant. Truth be told, it wasn't my idea, and I didn't even like the idea at the time. As much as I loved Megan's class chant (below) and thought the idea of it was cute, I didn't think chants or slogans mattered. So when Ms. Jackson asked me if she could begin to teach the students at CTS a chant that we'd use in hallways, in assemblies, and on playgrounds, I thought she was being overly-ambitious. I didn't stand in her way, but I didn't get in involved, especially because of how corny the chant actually was and the fact that it wasn't even proper English. It was a simple *call and response* chant. The call was "CTS." The response was "We Da Best."

Believe it or not, that terrible chant brought the school together like nothing I have ever seen before. Within a couple of weeks, all of the kids – even the too cool for school students – loved the chant. And, just like Ms. Jackson said, we ended up using it during assemblies, in hallways, and on the playgrounds. It actually turned out to be an amazing way to get students' attention. All I had to do – whether in a classroom, the cafeteria, on the playground, or in the parking lot – was yell "CTS" and miraculously, every student stopped what they were doing, yelled "We Da Best," and gave me their undivided attention.

When Megan started doing Roll Call at her monthly assemblies, she felt like something was missing. She reflected back to when she was in middle school. Every time they had an assembly, it always started with a school cheer that incorporated each grade's graduation year – *Ninety-seven! Ninety-seven! Fight, fight, fight for ninety-seven!* Megan decided that Norma Jones needed a school chant. Luckily, unlike me, she was pretty talented in this area. When she was a junior high teacher, she created a cheer for her homeroom to chant as they marched out to Field Day that her former students can still rehearse. It went: *We're the Gestsons! We're the Bestsons! We're better than the Restsons!* At Jones, it didn't take long for her to have a great cheer ready. Like most chants, it was nothing fancy, but it was something the kids would remember and be excited to shout.

> *Jo-Jo-Jo-Jo Jones! Jo-Jo-Jo-Jo Jones! Jo-Jo-Jo-Jo Jones!*
> *A little bit louder!*
> *Jo-Jo-Jo-Jo Jones! Jo-Jo-Jo-Jo Jones! Jo-Jo-Jo-Jo Jones!*
> *Couldn't be prouder!*
> *Jo-Jo-Jo-Jo Jones! Jo-Jo-Jo-Jo Jones! Jo-Jo-Jo-Jo Jones!*
> *Go Bulls!*

At Camelback, we had two *call and response* chants. The first was simple and had been used on and off throughout the years: the *call* was "CB" and the *response* was "HS." Since Phoenix Union has multiple schools that begin with "C," there is only one school in the district that is known as CHS – that's Central. All other "C" schools were given an alternative abbreviation – Camelback's was CBHS. Throughout all five years (and before and after), this served as the anchor *call and response* chant.

As for the second chant, we didn't create this until the second semester of my second year. It was a couple months after my major public proclamation that we were ridding Camelback of gangs, violence, and other disruptive behaviors. It was a difficult time, as we were focused more on eliminating negative behaviors than we were promoting positive ones. I decided it was time to start. So I had our staff identify 30 students who would be willing to lock themselves in a room with me for an entire day. Well, we weren't officially locked in, but we did spend the entire day in seclusion other than brief bathroom, stretch, and food breaks.

I had one agenda for the day – leave that room with 5-6 *core commitments* to which this group of 30 believed the entire student body could commit. My job was to simply facilitate, ask questions, and guide the group to a product. Aside from *core commitments*, we left that day with an unexpected product – a new school slogan that turned into a new chant. The slogan was, *Once a Spartan, Always a Spartan*. The students left that day so excited about the slogan that they began to teach it to their peers as a chant without my prompting. Eventually we taught it to the school at the next assembly, and it took off like wildfire. The *CB-HS* chant didn't go away – we just added a second option. Still to this day, when I run into a fellow Spartan, I often end the conversation with "Once a Spartan ..." and the former student always responds, "... Always a Spartan."

Engage, Excite, and Establish Expectations #39: Make Student Engagement Mandatory

In the mid-2000s, Johns Hopkins University produced a research article titled, *School Connectedness: Improving Student Lives*. They begin the article by saying, "Research has taught us that second only to family, school is the most important stabilizing force in the lives of young people." For many students today, as a result of family dynamics, school may actually be the primary place of stability. This is why school connectedness is extremely important for this generation of learners. Although the article lists several qualities of strong school connectedness, there are six relevant to this strategy:

1. Having a sense of belonging and being part of a school
2. Liking school
3. Perceiving that teachers are supportive and caring
4. Having good friends within school
5. Being engaged in their own current and future academic progress
6. Participating in extracurricular activities

What you see from this list is that connectedness, at its core, is about fostering a culture of student engagement – engagement with others (adults and peers), engagement in the school community, engagement with clubs and sports, and engagement in academics. Because the research is so clear that school connectedness plays a strong role in student achievement, principals must be willing to put forth significant effort to build systems and structures to ensure connectedness and engagement if they want to see significant academic gains over time.

I grew up in a suburb of Seattle that took high school football very seriously. Friday night football games were standing room only. You had to get there early if you wanted a good seat. The band and the student section were highly engaged. The crowd was nearly as intense as the players on the field. When I was offered the principalship at Camelback, I couldn't wait for that first Friday Night Lights experience. I knew the team wasn't strong (1-9 the last three seasons), but between the band, the students, and the crowd, I couldn't wait.

When I arrived, I have to admit, I was heartbroken. The band had less than 15 people. There were less than 50 people total in the stands – most were family and parents. The football team had about 30 players. There was no music during timeouts. No cheering during big plays. As if it couldn't get any worse, the few students who showed up were caught smoking pot in the bleachers and had to leave. That night, on my way home in the car, I told Megan, "As depressed as I am right now, I made a commitment to myself tonight that by the time I leave Camelback, we will have at least one night here with standing room only."

A few years later during Homecoming, with a revived football team, band, and school community, we not only had a standing room only crowd, we actually had to ask the band to move to make more room for the crowd. How did we do it? In part, it's because we made student engagement mandatory. Much like the idea of making academic success mandatory, we made school connectedness mandatory. At Camelback, we did it through the Spartan SHIELD that I mentioned earlier when I described Camelback's mission statement. The Spartan SHIELD was an acronym for the six characteristics every Spartan should embody as they walked across the stage at graduation. As you may recall, in order to ensure the SHIELD was not just a phrase on a mission statement but actually woven into the fabric of the school, students had to accomplish certain tasks or fulfill certain responsibilities to earn the SHIELD. Specifically, here were the requirements:

> **Stewardship:** In order to be a good steward of the community, every Spartan had to complete a certain number of community service hours per year.

> **Honor:** Honor at Camelback was two-fold. First, it was about being a respectful, honorable individual. Second, it was about honoring, respecting, and empathizing with others. To earn the "H" of the SHIELD, every Spartan had to honor the work of others by attending 10 campus events per year, from football games to dance recitals to a theatre performance. As we told our students, "No longer can you be a football player who expects everyone to come to your games.

You need to honor your peers by attending their events as well."

Intelligence: This component aligned directly with grades and Success Is Mandatory. In order to earn the "I," students had to pass their classes or successfully complete their mandatory tutoring hours.

Ethics: Being ethical at Camelback was about behavior and decision-making. Students had to receive no referrals, or show significant behavioral improvement throughout the year, to earn the "E."

Leadership: Participating in clubs and sports requires students to lead the self and others. To earn the "L," students had to participate in a club or a sport.

Discipline: Finally, Spartans were taught to be disciplined – disciplined thought, disciplined action. Students had to be responsible, organized, punctual. To earn the "D," students had to demonstrate discipline in the areas of homework, organization (of binders and agendas), attendance, and so forth. Determining successful completion of this component was the responsibility of the advisor.

There was a hidden agenda behind the Spartan SHIELD. The SHIELD was not simply about building stronger graduates, it was about systematically guaranteeing school connectedness. Connecting the SHIELD with advisory was also highly deliberate, as each student was assigned the same advisor for four years to guarantee each student had a caring adult on campus. What you'll see in the table below is that when we crosswalk advisory and the SHIELD with the research article above, there was intentional and direct alignment.

School Connectedness	Advisory and the Spartan SHIELD
Having a sense of belonging and being part of a school	Being a part of a club or a sport Attending campus events Completing community service hours on campus or in the community
Liking school	Engaging in a club or a sport of choice that aligns with a student's interest Having fun with peers at various school events throughout the year
Perceiving that teachers are supportive and caring	Having the same advisor all four years Connecting to a club sponsor or sports coach
Having friends in school	Having not only the same advisor but the same advisory peers all four years Meeting new friends in clubs and sports Attending campus events and completing community service hours with friends and peers

Being engaged in their own current and future academic progress	Being accountable for grades/Success Is Mandatory
	Being required to keep an organized binder, carry an agenda, complete homework, and track grades
Participating in extracurricular activities	Joining a club or sport
	Attending tutoring
	Using the library before and after school and on the weekends

The ultimate goal of the SHIELD was to create students who were highly connected, not for just for the sake of being engaged, but to drive achievement. Research is clear that students who are "connected" attend school more regularly, behave better, and experience more academic success than their peers who are not connected.

Connecting and engaging all students is no easy task. Despite all of these efforts, systems, structures, and programs, we were never able to connect all students. We still had students who failed more than one class. We still had students who didn't complete their community service requirement. We still had students who misbehaved, forgot their binders, and didn't join a club or sport. But we never gave up. One year, we identified a few hundred students who had still yet to join a club or a sport by the spring. So, we decided to start the "I Don't Have a Club Club." The goal of this club was not, in fact, to launch yet another club on campus. The idea was to connect them to other clubs and sports, knowing that most of these students just hadn't made the effort or took the risk to show up to a meeting or a practice. This club gave them the platform and support to do just that.

Of course, creating comprehensive systems to engage students in clubs, sports, community service, and campus events aligns well with high school life. Having such robust programming in elementary schools and middle schools may not be as possible or even as necessary. However, connectedness is important no matter the age or grade. Middle school students should be accountable for their own grades, their own progress, their own learning. Middle school students should be required to join clubs or sports. Middle school students should also be required to complete community service hours.

At CTS, all students had to complete a specific number of community service hours per year. Most of those hours were completed individually after school and on weekends. We did take the initiative to organize school-wide community service events with three goals. First, we wanted to remove any barriers that some students may have completing community service. Second, we know that a big part of service is working shoulder to shoulder with peers, developing new relationships, and strengthening old ones. Third, we wanted to clean up our community. Most of our weekend community service events were cleaning up alleys and empty lots and painting over graffiti.

In elementary schools, connectedness, though it may look and feel differently, is still critical. Elementary school students must learn to love school, and they must have at least one adult on campus who knows them and loves them authentically. They should also play a role in tracking their own academic progress. When I was an elementary school assistant principal, we even had first and second graders track the number of words they read per minute so that they could see and own their progress. Elementary school students should also feel connected to their peers which is why field days, homeroom competitions, and other fun activities are so important at any age.

Engage, Excite, and Establish Expectations #40: Bring College and Career to Life

Last but certainly not least, college and career. Although the original vision of public education in America was to create an educated populous that could sustain the democracy of America, education – like everything else in this nation – has evolved over time. Some things for the better. Others not. Producing an educated citizenry has and should always be one of the major goals of schooling in this country. Students must be taught to think, problem-solve, compromise, collaborate, and make educated and informed decisions. They should be taught history to better understand the future – to build off past successes and avoid repeating past failures. Students should also be encouraged to be *civicly engaged*, vote, and participate actively in the democracy of the 21st Century. But this can no longer be the only goal.

Our economy relies too heavily upon the K-12 system to produce the future workforce necessary to sustain our economy, not just our democracy. We are currently experiencing a major labor shortage in our country, and analysts predict that the shortages will get worse before they get better. Although schools may not necessarily be to blame for the crisis, they are undoubtedly a large part of the solution. The issue today is that in this accountability-driven and state label-obsessed season in education, schools don't allocate nearly enough time to getting students excited about and ready for college, career, and life. Schools have not only evolved away from recess, assemblies, and field trips, they've also shifted away from lessons and experiences that promote college and career.

In my personal experience as a leader, bringing college and

career to life for students has been one of the most impactful and even life-changing initiatives. The benefit is two-fold. First, according to most estimates, nearly two-thirds of all future careers will require some form of post-secondary education. It is an economic imperative that the school system graduates students who are focused on, and understand the importance of, college and career. Second, bringing college and career to life in the K-12 system enhances students' academic engagement and school connectedness. One of the main qualities of connectedness is monitoring future academic progress. This idea of tracking *future* academic progress is, in fact, helping students make connections to future college and career aspirations.

Earlier, I quoted one of the foundational beliefs of *Kids at Hope*, a non-profit that trains principals and teachers to view students from an *at hope* lens rather than an *at risk* lens. The *Kids at Hope* belief system is grounded in the school connectedness research and has three pillars: Believe, Connect, Time Travel. Within the Time Travel pillar, students are given a "passport to their future," teaching students to use "mental time travel" to envision their life in the future and how their decisions today impact their future.

Bringing College and Career to Life does just that. It starts to shape and frame the beliefs of the young men and the young women that we serve. For many students today in America, especially students of color or students who would become first generation college students, they cannot envision for themselves a brighter and better future without support, guidance, and opportunity. Recently, our district sent approximately 30 African-American students on a tour of Historically Black Colleges and Universities (HBCUs) in the south. One young woman, as she boarded the bus after the first visit, said to a chaperon. "I never really knew or believed that students like me went to college. Today, I saw myself everywhere. I now know that college is for me." That is why this Strategy is so important and impactful.

Bringing college and career to life is much more than hosting the typical Career Fair, although I still believe these are critically important as I'll share below. But we must look far beyond the usual Career Fair to help students envision for themselves a better future. Here are a few ways in which you can, and should, *Bring College and Career to Life* in schools.

Career Fair

As I said, Career Fairs are still relevant today. Exposing students to the usual careers as well as new and exciting careers and industries is important. There is still a large percentage of students who grow up dreaming of becoming a lawyer, a doctor, a firefighter, a police officer, and a nurse. Many students in lower-income communities haven't met or had an opportunity to interact with individuals from these industries. But as the world changes, so does the job market. It is also important to invite members from emerging fields – engineering, robotics, coding, and cyber security are great examples. Finally, do not forget the hands-on industries such as the construction trades. Today, a certified welder straight out of high school makes thousands more per year than teachers with Master's degrees. As wrong as that may sound, that's today's reality.

College and career are a huge part of the vision at Megan's school. Her Vision Team devotes a tremendous amount of time planning meaningful initiatives and activities focused on exposing students to opportunities after high school. Each May, her school hosts a Career Day, where more than 30 guest speakers come to present to the students. Speakers have represented careers in law, business, architecture, medicine, law enforcement, professional sports, construction, and technology. They even had the CEO of See's Candy one year.

Guest Speakers

As I mentioned in *Bring Back the Assembly*, I never hesitated to bring in guest speakers to talk about college, career, and life. When at all possible, I made sure that the demographics of our guest speakers mirrored those of our students. If you lead a primarily Latino community, find successful Latino leaders to tell their stories. If your school is low-income and full of future "first gen" college students, bring in young first gen college students or college graduates to share their journeys to and through college.

Banners and Pennants

Years ago, I read a research article on the differences between counseling offices in low-income schools versus counseling offices in middle- and upper-middle class schools. Counseling centers in low-income schools had walls full of posters promoting the military and trade schools. In more affluent neighborhoods, the walls were full of banners and pennants from local and elite colleges. One of the easiest ways to start a college-going culture is to fill your school with college paraphernalia. If you don't think you can afford to buy your own shirts, banners, posters, and pennants, do what we did at Camelback. I printed out lists of every single college and university in the country. I then divided up the list between various staff members – teachers, counselors, administrators. We all committed to emailing the Admissions Offices of these universities to ask them to send us anything they would be willing to send us for free. Within a month, we had enough college gear to fill the walls in the counseling center, the cafeteria, and the main commons area.

College Visits

Both Megan and I have always committed to allocating

funds, or doing private fundraising, to send kids on college tours. It doesn't cost that much money to rent a bus or two to send students to visit a college or university for a couple of hours. Many students in our country, especially those from low-income communities, have never experienced college. The act of simply walking on a college campus for the first time became the turning point for so many of our students over the years.

College Week

While at CTS, instead of one-off college visits and guest speakers, we organized an annual College Week. It was a huge, collective effort of the entire staff, as there were many components and activities throughout the week. As you'll see, College Week at CTS was truly designed to be transformational.

> **Theme:** Each year we chose a theme. That theme was then made into posters and banners that hung over doorways, in hallways, in the cafeteria, and on the marquee. The last year, our theme was simply, "From CTS to College."

> **Fight songs:** We taught students about college fight songs and then played them over the intercom during arrival, dismissal, and passing periods.

> **Decorations:** We spent a couple weeks the first year printing out and laminating hundreds of college logos. The weekend before College Week, we decorated the entire school with laminated banners of colleges and universities from throughout the country. Over the years, we acquired actual banners, pennants, and t-shirts that were hung in hallways and general areas throughout the campus.

Hats and Hoodies: All week, all staff wore shirts, hoodies, hats, and other clothing items to display their college pride. Teachers were encouraged to talk about their college(s) throughout the week as well.

Visits: Every single student visited a college during College Week. Every fifth grader visited a local community college on Monday. Sixth graders visited Arizona State University (our local university) on Tuesday. Seventh graders traveled up to the mountains to visit Northern Arizona University on Wednesday. Eighth graders drove across the state to the University of Arizona on Thursday.
While at the colleges, students had various tasks to complete. They did scavenger hunts. They ate lunch in the student union building. They usually met with a college recruiter or admissions specialist. When possible, they toured the dorms. Perhaps the most challenging yet rewarding was the requirement that they interview at least three random college students. We created questions ahead of time, so students just had to be brave enough to stop a student in the courtyard or in the student union to ask them a few questions. When students returned, they had to write about their experience during their English Language Arts, or ELA, class.

College Friday: College Week culminated with College Friday, a day where no content was taught because the entire day was set aside for college. Here's what the day looked like.

> **Morning Assembly:** We began the day with the first of two assemblies of the day. As students entered, college fight songs played over the speaker system. We showed pictures and videos

of colleges and universities from throughout the country. We talked about how amazing college is and why it is important. I then gave marching orders for the day.

Applications: For the next couple of hours, all students went back to the homerooms and applied to college. Of course, they didn't actually submit them, but they had to complete an entire college application, start to finish. What was most powerful about this experience was that they had to apply to college as if they were their 12th grade self. They had to assign themselves a GPA and the number of AP courses they took, list the clubs and sports they participated in, and think about the community service they would have completed.

Exemplary Personal Statements: We then spent about an hour learning about the importance of personal statements. We then had students read exemplary personal statements.

Personal Statement: After lunch, after having read exemplary personal statements, every student had to complete a personal statement. Again, as with the applications, students had to write their personal statement as if they were in 12th grade.

Final Assembly: We ended the day with a final assembly – the most exciting part of it all. Well in advance, every teacher at CTS was asked to create 2-3 exciting PowerPoint slides highlighting their college experience. They were encouraged to attach real pictures, tell real stories, and highlight real experiences. The stories had to be fun, funny, and/or inspirational. I then got up and gave the most inspirational closing possible – always with the central message being that every single one of them would go to and through college someday if they continued to work hard and be scholars.

The result of these college and career activities and experiences, not just College Week but this entire Strategy, is that students not only became more excited about college and life beyond school, but they also become more motivated to work hard and achieve in school. As *Kids at Hope* would say, we helped them *Time Travel* into their future and then, when they returned from their trip, we helped them create a roadmap back to that future.

Chapter 11
The 12 High Yield Strategies
A journey of a thousand miles begins with a single step ~ Chinese
Proverb

Do not let the 40 Strategies overwhelm you. You don't, can't, and shouldn't attempt to do them all at the same time. Even in the most ideal of situations, you can't and shouldn't attempt to complete all 40 in your first year. That's why I subtitled this book, *A Principal's Playbook to Year One **and Beyond***.

The easiest place to begin the journey is right at the beginning – with building relationships. If you start with *Memorizing Faces and Names* of your employees and then begin to *Know and Love Your Staff* by learning more about them as people, you'll find that the much of the rest takes care of itself. Take your time and pace yourself. Nobody wins an award for the fastest first mile in a marathon. In fact, if your first mile is too fast, you'll likely never see the finish line.

For those of you who aren't patient enough to strategically and methodically work your way through the Strategies, I have made a list of what I believe to be high-yield strategies. Obviously, I feel strongly that all 40 Strategies matter or else they wouldn't have made the cut. Candidly, I had many other strategies that I could have listed and even did in some cases in earlier drafts. But the 40 in the previous chapters are the most foundational and most impactful that I've experienced in my time in leadership.

What you may not have noticed in the Table of Contents is that I subtly highlighted 12 Strategies. I purposefully didn't draw too much attention to them, nor did I add any footnotes, as I wanted you read and experience all 40 before picking and choosing what works best for you. For that matter, even after you read through this list of 12 high-yield Strategies, you may have a different perspective. I encourage that. As I have mentioned several times throughout the course of this book, every single school and school leader is unique. Only you know what's best for you and your school community.

For me, here is a list of what I believe to be the 12 highest-yield Strategies:

Build Relationships
Strategy #2: Know and Love Your Staff

Enhance Your Institutional Knowledge
Strategy #7: Become the Chief Historian

Fix the Fixables (Don't Create Change)
Strategy #16: Focus on the Big 5
Strategy #17: Have Fun with Your Staff

Organize Leadership, Learning, and Listening Structures
Strategy #19: A Two-Team Approach
Strategy #22: Establish a Community Network

Review, Research, Reflect, Redesign
Strategy #25: Know What Exemplary Schools Are Doing (and Go Visit Them)

Engage, Excite, and Establish Expectations for Students
Strategy #29: Safe and Orderly
Strategy #36: Make It Cool to Be Smart
Strategy #37: Bring Back the Assembly
Strategy #39: Make Student Engagement Mandatory
Strategy #40: Bring College and Career to Life

Here is why I have chosen these. Relationship-building and knowing the history of a school are critically important. Without these, a school leader is flying solo and flying blindly – neither of which is safe or acceptable. If you can only find time to invest in a couple areas, getting to *Know and Love Your Staff* is low-energy, high-reward. If you make a conscious effort to learn a few key facts about every single employee, and use that information as a foundation for a relationship, you'll be off to a great start. Likewise, becoming the *Chief Historian* is the leadership equivalent of getting cataract surgery. Without having a thorough knowledge of the past and present of your school, you aren't seeing 20-20. Leaders need clear vision.

Although I could easily argue that *Finding Short-Term Wins* deserves to make the top 12, most of the early victories a leader would ever need can be found in the addressing the *Big 5*. Find one or two small improvements to the *Big 5* and you'll build both credibility and momentum. Often, building credibility also requires that you make strong connections with your staff. Knowing them and loving them is a great start. But *Having Fun with Your Staff*, allowing them to have fun with each other, and coordinating activities and experiences that build a sense of team and of family is essential to building a sense of community.

To take this sense of community to the next level, you must involve your staff in the decision-making as much as possible. Relying upon the traditional one-team approach of a site council or an academic leadership team will not yield the results for which you are looking. Instead, implement the *Two-Team Approach* – an academic leadership team and a non-academic leadership team – to increase leadership capacity, expedite the improvement process, and enhance buy-in, empowerment, and ownership.

As for the *Community Network*, I hesitated to make that a part of the 12 because it's a high-energy Strategy, yet it's also high-reward. Leaders need champions. Leaders need supporters. Leaders need resources. Leaders also need mentors, guides, and thought-partners. A *Community Network* can provide all of these. Your network doesn't have to be huge at the outset. Find 5-6 local community members to get started – an attorney, a few business owners, and a couple dedicated community members. Meet with them monthly and share your goals, your challenges, your successes, and your struggles. Eventually have them invite a respected and trusted friend or colleague to join the group. Before you know it, you'll have a highly engaged *Community Network* committed to your (and your school community's) success.

Although every step in the ***Review, Research, Reflect, Redesign*** phase is important, if I had to pick one Strategy that would energize and motivate your teams more than any other, it would be to study and visit exemplary schools. Read a few national case studies. Identify a couple local schools who are beating the odds or exceeding the standards, arrange for a couple-hour visit, and bring a small team that is ready to listen and learn.

Choosing just a handful of the twelve ***Engage, Excite, and Establish Expectations for Students*** Strategies was surely the most difficult. After all, we are in this business to do just that – implement systems, structures, programs, and activities that transform the lives of youth. All school reform and school improvement must begin with guaranteeing a *Safe and Orderly* campus. This always has to be priority number one.

One of the best ways to promote good behavior, work ethic, and achievement is to publicly lift up and recognize the students who do it best. If I had to pick one Strategy from this entire book, it would unquestionably be *Make It Cool to Be Smart*. Although I listed nearly 10 ways in which you can make this happen, start with developing a robust Honor Roll and watch the culture of your school begin to change almost instantly. Speaking of changing culture, this is virtually an impossible task without getting your entire school community together to laugh, to celebrate, to set expectations, to recognize. *Bring Back the Assembly* is not only **not** a waste of instructional time, it actually improves instructional time.

Aside from rigor and high expectations, research finds that student connectedness is one of the leading factors contributing to student achievement. When you get to a focus *on* teaching and learning, you can concentrate on rigor and high expectations. For now, get your students connected. Institute a school-wide community service requirement. Implement an advisory or house system if you lead a middle school or high school. Train your teachers to know and love your kids to ensure that every student has a caring adult on campus with whom they connect consistently.

Students also need to make connections to their future. Career Fairs, College Weeks, college visits and guest speakers help students visualize themselves in college and in a career. This is especially important for students of color and first generation students. This image of their future provides for them a sense of hope and also translates into increased focus and commitment in the classroom.

Regardless of which Strategies you employ – all 40, these 12, or others that resonated with you – implement them with intentionality and fidelity. Make sure that your staff, including your two leadership teams, play a significant role in executing, monitoring, and adjusting any strategy or initiative that you employ. And, as Strategy #18 reminds us, be patient, be thoughtful, and be disciplined.

Final Reflections

I pen these final words in the spring time in Phoenix, Arizona. It's one of the most beautiful times of the year here. There is no more threat of frost or freeze that kill certain desert foliage – yes, Phoenix freezes a few times each winter. The mornings and evenings in the spring have less of a bite and the daily temperature continues to rise. Before we know it, we will be in triple digits for four months. For the gardeners in the Valley of the Sun, the onset of spring means it is prime gardening season.

Megan is the gardener of the family. I am by no means gardening-adverse – I love yard work and, as a fourth generation carpenter, love using my hands whenever possible. But the actual act of gardening is Megan's area. She selects the soil, the seeds, the plants. I am simply responsible for demolishing old gardens and re-building new ones when and where she tells me. I buy the materials, haul the materials, and install the materials. I guess you can say that I am the brawns of the operations. Megan is definitely the brains.

If you don't have a green thumb, you may not know that gardening is a highly complex art and science. To start, gardens must be placed in the perfect location with the right balance of direct sunlight and shading. The soil must be perfect, a blend of topsoil, manure, and other nutrients that help plants thrive in the region in which they are planted. The depth of the soil has to be just right as well – too shallow and the seeds won't survive, too deep and the water saturation won't be right. Sunlight and shade are also critical. Too much sun and the seed dries out and dies long before it sprouts. Too much shade and the seed never fulfills its ultimate purpose. The seasons matter as well. The temperature and the hours of daylight all contribute to a healthy, or not-so-healthy, garden. There are also plants that can only thrive in the summer yet die in the winter. There are plants that can thrive in the winter yet shrivel up in the summer. There are also seeds and plants that need more sun while others need less.

It is only after months of calculated gardening – the right soil, right sun, right moisture, right conditions – that a gardener reaps the harvest and bears the fruits (and vegetables) of his or her labor.

The *BEFORE Teaching and Learning* model is all about reaping a harvest at the right time. Leaders who go too fast, focus solely on test scores and state labels, ignore relationships and the research on human psychology and motivation, and forget that they are in the business of people, not just the student achievement business, often have short-lived, tenuous tenures that yield short-term, unsustainable growth. Without the right preparation – without the right soil – it does not matter what programs, procedures, and initiatives a leader tries to implement, the results – the growth – won't occur.

There is a biblical scripture in the fourth chapter of Mark that provides for us a perfect and very secular image of the importance of planting seeds in healthy soil and in the right conditions. This is known as the Parable of the Sower:

> "A sower went out to sow. And as he sowed, some seed fell along the path, and the birds came and devoured it. Other seed fell on rocky ground, where it did not have much soil, and it immediately sprang up, since it had no depth of soil. And when the sun rose, it was scorched, and since it had no root, it withered away. Other seed fell among thorns, and the thorns grew up and choked it, and it yielded no grain. And other seeds fell into good soil and produced grain, growing and increasing and yielding thirtyfold and sixtyfold and a hundredfold."

This parable provides for us four powerful leadership lessons, all aligned perfectly with the overarching philosophy and beliefs inherent in the BEFORE Teaching and Learning framework.

"And as he sowed, some seed fell along the path, and the birds came and devoured it."

Too many leaders today have such a strong desire (and feel pressure and accountable) for great academic achievement and "Exemplary" or "A" state labels that they begin spreading seeds of change immediately without first building relationships and prepping the soil. People are naturally-change adverse and without the proper preparation, they will, much like the birds, devour and destroy you and any initiative you try to implement.

"Other seed fell on rocky ground, where it did not have much soil, and it immediately sprang up, since it had no depth of soil. And when the sun rose, it was scorched, and since it had no root, it withered away."

Other leaders, out of impatience, plant the seeds of change after just a few weeks of relationship-building. At first, it may seem like the timing is right – a small group of people with whom the leader has made connections appear to be ripe for change. But this is misleading. A leader needs more than just a few followers. Shortly after implementation, the change withers and dies because the soil wasn't yet ready.

"Other seed fell among thorns, and the thorns grew up and choked it, and it yielded no grain."

Many leaders implement changes in isolation, without feedback or input from others, and without teams of dedicated stakeholders helping with planning, implementation, and monitoring. Even if the changes have the potential to be effective, without buy-in, empowerment, and ownership, the change will be choked by the thorns of a staff and a community that don't have the level of commitment necessary to make the changes take root.

"And other seeds fell into good soil and produced grain, growing and increasing and yielding thirtyfold and sixtyfold and a hundredfold."

Great leaders – leaders who subscribe to relationship-building, informed decision-making, and shared leadership – only plant the seeds of change in soil that is ripe and ready for explosive growth. Leaders who properly cultivate the soil always reap the harvest in due time. The Parable of the Sower – one of the greatest leadership lessons ever written.

2,000 years later ...

As a college student in Seattle, as Megan and I made our way to the local grocery store, we drove by an elderly gentleman who was struggling mightily to mow his own lawn. It wasn't a large lawn by any means, but his age, his health, and an obvious disability made this task extremely painful to observe. I couldn't imagine the physical pain he must have experienced pushing that old rusty lawn mower across the lawn. I could see it in his face.

I commented to Megan as we drove by, "I think I am supposed to offer to mow that man's lawn for him."

We then proceeded to discuss the many reasons why that probably wasn't a reasonable thought. His yard was likely a point of pride for him. Mowing was probably his only form of exercise. I was a full-time student *and* worked full-time in the construction trade. Surely I didn't have the time to mow someone's lawn every couple of weeks.

After completing our shopping and running a few more errands, we passed back by his house about an hour later. There was that man, sitting on his front steps, admiring his lawn. Megan and I couldn't decide if he was proud or exhausted. I guessed the latter.

For a week, I couldn't get the image of the man out of my head and, despite the many reasons why it would be an impractical idea, I swung by his house one morning on the way to work and dropped off a note.

> "Good morning, Sir.
> I drove by your house a week ago as you were mowing your lawn. I feel called to at least offer. I would be more than willing to come by your home every other week to take care of your lawn for you. I don't need, nor would I accept, any money. If you have any interest in my assistance, my number is below."

Within a couple of hours, I received a phone call from John's wife, Betsy. She said that my letter was "divine intervention" and came at the perfect time. John's health was declining quickly, and she had just told him earlier that week that she needed to find someone to take care of the lawn for fear he would drop dead if he had to do it again. They had no family in town to help and couldn't afford a real landscaping service.

For the next several months, I made the short trip to John and Betsy's house to mow their lawn. John would sit on the front steps as I mowed the front yard and then would move to the back deck as I mowed the back. Every day when I finished, they invited me into their living room, handed me a glass of water, and, despite my opposition, gave me a $10 bill that I then donated to the local church. In that living room which appeared to be stuck in the 1950s, John told me the same stories over and over again every other week as Betsy sat by listening intently as if she was hearing the stories for the first time. He was an army veteran, an engineer, and a master gardener.

Although still to this day, I do not garden and surely do not like tomatoes, John shared with me the perfect process for growing the most flawless, red, ripe, juicy tomato. As it turns out, it has nothing to do with the seed. And it has everything to do with the soil.

Notes

Chapter 2
Every Child Succeeds Act. https://www.ed.gov/essa?src=rn

Chapter 3
Principal Turnover Takes Costly Toll on Students and Districts.
Superville, Denisa. Published November 5, 2014, at
https://edweek.org
Microsoft. https://www.microsoft.com/en-us/about
Google. https://www.google.com/intl/en/about/our-company/
Southwest Airlines.
https://www.southwest.com/html/about-southwest/index.html?clk=GFOOTER-ABOUT-ABOUT
Why Do Southwest Airlines Employees Always Seem So Happy.
July 28, 2017.
https://www.forbes.com/sites/darrendahl/2017/07/28/why-do-southwest-airlines-employees-always-seem-so-happy/#af8508059b0e

Chapter 4
Elmore, Richard. *School Reform from the Inside Out: Policy,*
Practice, and Performance. 2004. Harvard Education Press.
Massachusetts.
Collins, Jim. *Good to Great: Why Some Companies Make the Leap*
and Others Don't. 2001. Harper. New York.

Chapter 5
Kouzes, James and Posner, Barry. 2017. *The Leadership*
Challenge: How to Make Extraordinary Things Happen in
Organizations. John Wiley and Sons, Inc. New Jersey.
Boyatzis, Richard, Goleman, Daniel, and McKee, Annie. 2013.
Primal Leadership: Unleashing the Power of Emotional Intelligence.
Harvard Business School Publishing. Massachusetts.

Maxwell, John. 2007. *The 21 Irrefutable Laws of Leadership: Follow Them and People Will Follow You.* Thomas Nelson. Tennessee.

Chapman, Bob and Sisodia, Raj. 2015. *Everybody Matters: The Extraordinary Power of Caring for Your People Like Family.* Penguin Random House. New York.

Starbucks. https://www.starbucks.com/about-us/company-information

Uber. https://www.uber.com/about/

Lyft. https://www.lyft.com/about

Chapter 6

Harkins Theatres. https://www.harkins.com/harkins-history/red

Thinking Maps. https://www.thinkingmaps.com/

Chapter 7

Ten Reasons People Resist Change. Rosabeth Moss Kanter. Harvard Business Review. www.hbr.com. Published September 25, 2012 at https://hbr.org/2012/09/ten-reasons-people-resist-chang

Achor, Shawn. 2010. *The Happiness Advantage: The Seven Principles of Positive Psychology that Fuel Success and Performance at Work.* Crown Publishing Group. New York.

Heath, Chip and Heath, Dan. 2010. *Switch: How to Change Things When Change Is Hard.* Crown Publishing Group. New York.

Kotter, John. 2012. *Leading Change.* Harvard Business Review Press. Massachusetts.

Black, Conrad. 2013. Franklin Delano Roosevelt: Champion of Freedom. Public Affairs. New York.

Giuliani, Rudolph. 2002. *Leadership.* Hyperion. New York.

Target. https://www.target.com/

Pictionary. http://www.mattelgames.com/en-us/family/pictionary

Jeopardy. https://www.jeopardy.com/

The Amazing Race.
https://www.cbs.com/shows/amazing_race/

Chapter 8

Dirkswager, Edward and Farris-Berg, Kim. 2013. *Trusting Teachers with School Success: What Happens When Teachers Call the Shots*. The Rowman and Littlefield Publishing Group, Inc. Maryland.

Degrees of Distribution: Towards an Understanding of Variations in the Nature of Distributed Leadership in Schools. Ritchie, Ron and Woods, Phillip. Published August 28, 2007 at https://www.tandfonline.com/doi/abs/10.1080/1363243070 1563130

When Teachers Run the School. Giouroukakis, Vicky and Natsiopoulou, Eleni. Educational Leadership. www.ascd.com. Published April 2010 at http://www.ascd.org/publications/educational-leadership/apr10/vol67/num07/When-Teachers-Run-the-School.aspx

Success Is Mandatory. www.successismandatory.com

The Ritz-Carlton. http://www.ritzcarlton.com/en/about

The Breakthrough Coach. http://www.the-breakthrough-coach.com/home

Camelback Montessori College Preparatory and Camelback Virtual. www.camelbackhs.org

Social Venture Partners. http://www.socialventurepartners.org/who-we-are/

Circle K. https://www.circlek.com/

Subway. http://www.subway.com/en-us/aboutus/history

Panda Express. https://www.pandaexpress.com/

Camelback Gap Scholarship Fund. https://www.azfoundation.org/Scholarships/ScholarshipFu nds/CamelbackHighSchoolScholarshipFund.aspx

Peer Power Foundation. http://www.peerpowerfoundation.org/

Greenberg Traurig Law Firm. https://www.gtlaw.com/en

Chapter 9

Blanchard, Kenneth and Johnson, Spencer. 1998. *Who Moved My Cheese?: An Amazing Way to Deal with Change in Your Work and in Your Life.* G. P. Putnam's Sons Publishers. New York.

Penny, Louise. 2008. *Still Life.* St. Martin's Press. New York.

A Theory of Human Motivation. 1943. A.H. Maslow. Complete manuscript can be found at http://psychclassics.yorku.ca/Maslow/motivation.htm

Why Change Programs Don't Produce Change. Beer, Michael, Eisenstat, Russell, and Spector, Bert. Published on November, 1990, at https://hbr.org/1990/11/why-change-programs-dont-produce-change

NCAA Clearinghouse. http://www.ncaa.org/student-athletes/future/eligibility-center

Informed Decision Making in Outpatient Practice. Clarence H. Braddock III, MD, MPH; Kelly A. Edwards, MA; Nicole M. Hasenberg, MPH; et al. Published on December 22, 1999 at https://jamanetwork.com/journals/jama/fullarticle/192233

Hot Cheetos. https://www.fritolay.com/snacks/product-page/cheetos/cheetos-crunchy-flamin-hot-cheese-flavored-snacks

Bureau of Labor Statistics. Published March 27, 2018 at https://www.bls.gov/emp/chart-unemployment-earnings-education.htm

Sizer, Theodore. 2004. *Breaking Ranks II: Strategies for Leading High School Reform.* National Association of Secondary School Principals. www.nassp.com. Virginia.

Lemov, Doug. 2015. *Teach Like a Champion: 62 Techniques that Put Students on a Path to College.* Josey-Bass. California.

Medina, John. 2014. *Brain Rules: 12 Principals for Surviving and Thriving at Work, Home, and School.* Pear Press. Washington.

Black, Paul, Harrison, Chris, and Lee, Clare, et.al. 2004. *Assessment for Learning: Putting it into Practice.* McGraw-Hill. New York.

Brown-Chidsey, Rachel and Steege, Mark. 2011. *Response to Intervention: Principles and Strategies for Effective Practice.* Guliford Press. New York.

Advanced Placement. https://ap.collegeboard.org/

School Connectedness: Strategies for Increasing Protective Factors Among Youth. Centers for Disease Control and Prevention. www.cdc.gov. Published 2009 at https://www.cdc.gov/healthyyouth/protective/pdf/connectedness.pdf

Correlates of Effective Schools: The First and Second Generation. 1999. Lezotte, Lawrence. Published at https://www.gulllakecs.org/cms/lib/MI01001276/Centricity/Domain/65/Correlates_of_Effective_Schools.pdf

Lezotte, Lawrence. 2010. *What Effective Schools Do: Re-Envisioning the Correlates.* Solution Tree. Indiana.

Nine Characteristics of High-Performing Schools: A Research-Based Resource for Schools and Districts to Assist with Improving Student Learning. Second Edition, 2007. Published at http://www.k12.wa.us/research/pubdocs/NineCharacteristics.pdf

Pinnacle High School. https://www.pvschools.net/phs

Greater Phoenix Leadership. https://www.gplinc.org/

Why Looping Is a Way Underappreciated School Improvement Initiative. Minkel, Justin. Published on June 17, 2015 at https://www.edweek.org/tm/articles/2015/06/17/looping-a-way-underappreciated-school-improvement-initiative.html

Collins, Jim and Hansen, Morten. 2011. *Great by Choice.* Harper Collins Publishing. New York.

Maxwell, John. 2007. *Failing Forward: Turning Mistakes into Stepping Stones for Success.* Thomas Nelson Publishing. Tennessee.

Seven Reasons Your Company Needs a Clear, Written Mission Statement. Glenn Smith. Published on March 29, 2016 at http://www.glennsmithcoaching.com/7-reasons-your-company-needs-clear-written-mission-statement/

The Nine Worst Mission Statements of All Time. Zetlin, Minda. Published on November 15, 2013 at https://www.inc.com/minda-zetlin/9-worst-mission-statements-all-time.html
Avon. https://www.avon.com/
Albertsons. https://www.albertsons.com/#1
MGM Resorts. https://www.mgmresorts.com/en.html
Dell. http://www.dell.com/en-us

Chapter 10
Kids at Hope. http://kidsathope.org/who-we-are/
Boys Town. http://www.boystowntraining.org/
Make Your Day. http://www.aboutmakeyourday.com/
The School to Prison Pipeline: Practices and Policies that Favor Incarceration Over Education Do Us All a Grave Injustice. Elias, Marilyn. Published 2013 at https://www.tolerance.org/magazine/spring-2013/the-schooltoprison-pipeline
The Arizona Department of Education. www.azed.gov
Centre for Justice and Reconciliation. http://restorativejustice.org/about-us/mission-vision-and-values/#sthash.XleQKnwk.dpbs
Bible. https://www.bible.com/
Gatorade. https://www.gatorade.com/
You Can't Fire Your Way to Success. Kettl, Donald. Published January 2018 at https://www.govexec.com/excellence/promising-practices/2018/01/you-cant-fire-your-way-success/145618
Playworks. https://www.playworks.org/about/
The Power of I Love You from Dad. Published at http://www.fathers.com/s12-championship-fathering/the-power-of-i-love-you-from-dad/
Merriam Webster. https://www.merriam-webster.com/dictionary/love
How to Be a Good Parent. https://www.wikihow.com/Be-a-Good-Parent.

Seattle Seahawks. https://www.seahawks.com/

Gladwell, Malcolm. 2011. *Outliers: The Story of Success*. Hachette Book Group. New York.

Gladwell, Malcolm. 2007. *Blink: The Power of Thinking Without Thinking*. Hachette Book Group. New York.

Gladwell, Malcom. 2002. *Tipping Point: How Little Things Can Make a Big Difference*. Hachette Book Group. New York.

Harvard University. https://www.gse.harvard.edu/ppe/program/national-institute-urban-school-leaders

Rachel's Challenge. https://rachelschallenge.org/

The City of Phoenix. https://www.phoenix.gov/nsd/programs/graffiti

School Connectedness: Improving Student Lives. Blum, Robert. Published in 2004 at https://www.casciac.org/pdfs/SchoolConnectedness.pdf

Education to the Masses: The Rise of Public Education in Early America. Brackemyre, Ted. Published in 2012 at http://ushistoryscene.com/article/rise-of-public-education/

Carnevale, Anthony, Smith, Nicole and Strohl, Jeff. *Recovery*. Published at https://cew.georgetown.edu/wp-content/uploads/2014/11/Recovery2020.ES_.Web_.pdf

A National Look at the High School Counseling Office: What It Is Doing and What Role It Can Play in Facilitating Students' Path to College. Lew, Terry, Ifill, Nicole and Radford, Alexandria Walton. National Association for College Admissions Counseling. Pubslished at https://www.nacacnet.org/globalassets/documents/publications/research/hsls_counseling.pdf

Historically Black Colleges and Universities. https://sites.ed.gov/whhbcu/one-hundred-and-five-historically-black-colleges-and-universities/

Arizona State University. https://www.asu.edu/

Northern Arizona State University. https://nau.edu/

University of Arizona. http://www.arizona.edu/